BEYOND YOUR OWNERSHIP

How Employee Ownership Can Align Your Purpose, People, and Profit

Bob Whalen

With Jamie Dykstra

Beyond Your Ownership
How Employee Ownership Can Align Your Purpose, People, and Profit

Published by Reflek Publishing

Disclaimer: The author makes no guarantees concerning the level of success you may experience by following the advice and strategies contained in this book, and you accept the risk that results will differ for each individual. The purpose of this book is to educate, entertain, and inspire.

For more information: beyondownership@hb-global.com

ISBN: 978-1-968164-17-1 (paperback)
ISBN: 978-1-968164-18-8 (ebook)

I dedicate this book to my partner in
chasing my true purpose.

Mandy, I love you!

Table of Contents

Preface

On a particularly frigid Chicago day in January 2019, our Master of Finance class filed into a modest classroom at the University of Notre Dame's satellite Chicago campus. Having already spent a week in South Bend together, we had been assigned our groups and gotten some of the "first day of school" jitters out.

We began to jockey for tables to sit with our groups or other friends we'd made during our first immersion week. My group of four found an empty table so we could all sit together, but that left one empty chair... Little did I know that the fifth member to join our table would cross paths with me for many years to come.

Bob Whalen filled that last seat at our table for the whole year that we spent in the program together. While much of our time was spent with our groups, I got to know Bob a little bit. We'd chat about his kids, how his travels from Pennsylvania were, sports, etc. Early in the school year, Notre Dame released an article on Bob and how he'd transitioned the company he'd bought to being employee-owned. Bob was also given the opportunity to chat more about this with our class. I thought it was pretty cool, but admittedly didn't think much of it at the time. I was immersed in the corporate world and my plight to climb the corporate ladder, using my Master of Finance degree as ammunition.

Bob kept a pretty low profile throughout the year. I knew he ran an HVAC company and that he was generally an overall good guy. He seemed to know his stuff and have a wealth of knowledge and experience.

Our cohort wrapped up classes in December 2019, celebrated with a champagne toast overlooking the Chicago skyline, and went on our way, planning to reconvene at the graduation ceremony on campus in May 2020.

It will come as no shock that the ceremony was postponed due to the COVID-19 pandemic and rescheduled for May 2021. It was then postponed again as cases surged in the Spring of 2021. Finally, in May 2022, we'd get our chance to celebrate our graduation on campus. But with two and a half years between the end of the program and the ceremony, turnout was light. Bob was among those missing from the graduation he had looked forward to, so he could attend his son's collegiate baseball games.

During that time period, my life was beginning to shift. I left the corporate world in April 2022. After some time to reflect, I knew I wanted to start my own business, but I wasn't even sure what I could excel at outside of corporate finance and operations. A dear friend suggested that I was good at writing and could try my hand at that. Unsure at first but wanting to gain some traction, I gave it a go.

After exploring some different avenues, I started a copywriting business in the Fall of 2023. Shortly after posting a blog about copywriting, I saw a calendar invite pop up in my inbox from Bob Whalen. I was thrilled! I had genuinely enjoyed being classmates with Bob and was happy to reconnect and potentially help him and his business through my work.

I figured I should do some research on his company to prepare for the meeting. I knew he ran an HVAC company in Pennsylvania but didn't know much beyond that. I dove in, and my jaw dropped further and further to the ground as I combed through the HB Global family of brands and other company information. True to Bob's personality and character, he had never alluded to the size and scope of his company.

As I dug into different resources, including Bob's podcast *Employee Ownership with Bob Whalen*, I learned more and more about ESOPs (Employee Stock Ownership Plans). I had heard of ESOPs before but really didn't know much about them. I was happy if I could just remember what the acronym stood for. By the end of my research on HB Global, I was fired up about the concept of employee ownership because of all it could accomplish for individual employee owners and companies alike.

Bob and I chatted over a few Zoom calls about the ways that we could partner together to support his company. We put together an agreement, and I got to work.

On one of the first calls, I mentioned to him that he could write an amazing book advocating for the power of employee ownership. He said he'd considered it, that it may happen at some point, and pretty much left it at that.

Months passed, and I continued to support HB Global in their strategic communications. Concurrently, however, I'd also added non-fiction book ghostwriting to my service offerings. I mentioned the idea of partnering with Bob on a book, and he again said he was considering it, but the conversation stayed put for some time. In the meantime, I partnered with other thought leaders on their book projects, as this offering moved into the forefront of my business

As we neared the end of 2024, Bob gave me a call and said he thought he was ready to write a book. Despite the words he was saying, I could still sense a bit of hesitation. I walked him through what the process would look like, the timelines, and the investment. We talked about what direction he'd potentially like to see the book go, but I could still sense some resistance. Finally, Bob came out with it.

He told me he was hesitant to write a book because he didn't want it to seem as if he was partaking in some sort of self-promotion. He didn't want to appear as if he was just building up his ego by having his name on the cover of a book. Classic Bob.

I explained to him that writing this book would be an act of service. By authoring a book, he'd be amplifying the reach of employee ownership beyond what he could do without this tool. This book would create awareness of a solution that many business owners may not even know exists. I told him that it would be another powerful asset to help him fulfill his professional purpose. With that, he was on board.

We spent the next several months working together on this project, along with Sara Kann, VP Chief of Staff at HB Global, who provided additional support and insights. After mapping out the initial goals for the book and the outline, we'd spend each week in interviews. What a treat this was for me, getting to learn all about employee ownership from Bob and hear stories of how it had truly changed lives. I also had the opportunity to gain insights into Bob's leadership philosophies and values.

While working through the interviews, I got to work on writing. As a ghostwriter, I get the opportunity to put "pen to paper" on an author's thought leadership and voice. What you see throughout this book is fully and authentically Bob's. It's his voice, it's his views, it's his stories... It's his professional mission coming to life.

After the first draft was completed, Bob pored over it, ensuring that it accurately captured his views, beliefs, and general essence. In true Bob fashion, he also solicited the feedback of members of his family, team, and other trusted colleagues to gain additional perspectives and thoughts. The book has gone through multiple iterations, and the result that you see is a true reflection of Bob.

While atypical for a ghostwriter (and certainly not expected), Bob wanted to give recognition to my role in the process. When he first mentioned having my name out in the open, I was speechless. I don't do my work for recognition but rather to make an impact through bringing powerful thought leadership to life. That being said, I couldn't have been more thrilled, and it is my absolute great honor to be recognized as a collaborator on this book.

I am deeply grateful for the opportunity to have worked with Bob and his team on this project to raise awareness for such an important, yet underutilized, business structure. Employee ownership truly has the opportunity to change lives, and it's my great privilege to play a small part in advocating for it.

My hope for you is that after reading this book, you are as fired up about employee ownership as I was after learning about it from Bob. I am eager to see the awareness of it grow through the work that Bob, his team, and so many great organizations do.

With Gratitude,

Jamie Dykstra
August 2025

Introduction

I want every employee who works with our company to be a millionaire by the time they retire. While this may sound like a lofty goal, we're on track to make that happen.

This commitment of mine is not filled with empty promises. It's largely made possible by my decision to transition our company to an ESOP (Employee Stock Ownership Plan).

****

Our Board of Directors looked at me like I was nuts. Why would I want to set myself up to potentially be fired? This is how the conversation went as I pitched the idea of transitioning HB McClure to an ESOP in 2010. So... why did I want to make that switch?

In April of 2008, I joined HB McClure by purchasing 7.5% of the company. HB McClure was an HVAC company local to the Harrisburg, PA area with about 150 employees that performed residential and commercial maintenance, replacement, and construction. When I joined, we were in the midst of a record year. Well, we all know what happened in 2008 – we were in recession and didn't know it. As the year progressed, the performance of the business had already started to deteriorate. It was like a train wreck waiting to happen.

After my 7.5% purchase on Day 1, the plan had been for me to buy the rest of the company over the next six to seven years using the cash flows generated from the business. This set up was a win-win because it gave me some time to purchase the entire company while being structured to set Bob McClure, the seller of the company, up for retirement. Bob was perfectly willing to be patient with the payments if we weren't able to make them because of financial performance, but I could see the inefficiencies happening from drawing out this plan.

In my mind, drawing out the process would be an inefficient use of resources, ultimately impacting our employees. So I set out to find a way to honor the structure of the original deal we had set up without unnecessarily burdening the employees. Basically, I went looking to try to make the deal cheaper. One way to do this was through taxes. Our first deal was incredibly tax-inefficient because we were using all post-tax dollars to make it happen. As I researched ways to make the transaction more affordable, I came across the ESOP structure. If we structured the company this way, there would be no income tax to pay going forward for the portion of the company that was structured as an ESOP, which would give us more capital to work with during the transition period.

So our new plan was to make the company 100% ESOP-owned, where Bob McClure held ⅔ of the debt and the bank held ⅓ of the debt. This created a more efficient deal, which allowed for more resources to stay in the company and ultimately benefit our employees with more free cash flow, the ability to purchase new tools and equipment, pay higher salaries and bonuses, and more.

While the ESOP setup was more tax efficient and solved for the structure originally agreed upon, it also ultimately aligned with the cultural goals I wanted for the business. It was the perfect solution for us.

So I went to the Board to make this pitch, and they basically told me I was crazy. I had a chance to own 100% of the company with the prior owner willing to be patient with payments, and I was going to pass that up for employees to share in the ownership of the company! Furthermore, the Board would need to transition from being an advisory board to being a fiduciary board. This exposed me to potentially being fired one day if the fiduciaries of the company felt my being in the CEO seat wasn't in the best interest of the company.

But I persisted. I felt the resources that were going to be freed up were important enough. I felt what this structure did for our company culturally and financially were important enough. And I didn't, and still don't, mind being held accountable for our results as the CEO. What was most important to me was running this iconic Harrisburg-based company. I would've done it as an employee. Saying I owned the company wasn't crazy important to me.

But besides all these tactical business reasons to go about structuring the company as an ESOP, I'll admit that I had some personal reasons as well. I had my four kids' college educations to pay for on the horizon, and I was going to need the cash flow to cover that. Because of how the deal was structured, I received more cash compensation in the short-term as well. The efficiency we were creating was a benefit to both me and the employees.

Despite all the reasoning and explanation I gave, the Board still thought I was nuts, but they went along with it. So our next step was to go to the employees and explain the transition the company would be making to an employee-owned business.

I was very open with the employees. I explained to them the important benefits of the transition and the value they would get from it both financially and culturally. I was also very open with them that while this structure perfectly aligned with my cultural goals for the company that I wasn't a saint. I would benefit from it as well.

At the time, we decided to structure the business as an ESOP because of the financial stress of the economic environment. There were several reasons we needed to be more efficient, including creating more capital for the transition and efficiently using our resources for the benefit of our company and employees. I could see the short-term benefits, and the long-term benefits were clear in theory. What I didn't realize at the time was that employee ownership would become a passion of mine and that advocating for it would become my professional mission.

****

I've been with the company for 17 years now and have never once questioned what I've done with my life. So often, climbing the ladder in the business world comes with financial rewards but also sacrifices that make executives question "for whom" and "for what" they've invested all this time and energy. Those questions have never crossed my mind. Patrick O'Shaughnessy defines "Life's Work" as "a lifelong quest to build something for others that expresses who you are."[1] This perfectly captures what an ESOP company is for me.

In 14 years of being an ESOP, we've gone from an enterprise value of approximately $5 million to an enterprise value of approximately $320 million, including an ESOP value of over $200 million as of September 30, 2024. In 2017 we formed a parent company called HB Global that currently houses 12 subsidiaries (including HB McClure) with about 1,700 employees completing work across the US and beyond (as of 2024). Our subsidiaries focus on service, replacement, and construction in the commercial, residential, and infrastructure markets. I'm proud of this growth and the benefits that have been passed on to our employee owners. With this level of success, I'd also be the prime person who could question why I decided to structure the business as an ESOP instead of walking out to my helicopter.

The truth is, you can have your cake and eat it, too. As I set out on my ownership journey, I had developed compensation projections so that I'd be able to comfortably retire at 65. At the age of 55, I am well ahead of those projections as the leader of an ESOP business. I'm financially

[1] @patrick_oshag (Patrick Oshaughnessy), "My definition of 'Life's Work:' 'A lifelong quest to build something. . .,'" X.com, August 12, 2023, at 12:25 PM, https://x.com/patrick_oshag/status/1690444379494690816?lang=en.

secure and sleep easy at night knowing our employees are taken care of in both the long-term and short-term. I never have regrets or question how I've spent my career as a CEO.

This freeing feeling has lit my passion for employee ownership, and I'm on a mission to create awareness for others of the availability of this structure. Is it right for everyone? No. And my goal isn't to force this on any owner or leader. I do, however, want widespread awareness of the potential to utilize this structure when it makes sense and aligns with an owner's intentions.

****

While raising awareness of the power of ESOPs and creating immense value for our employee owners is now my primary professional mission, I recognize that this passion has been fueled by my life's journey. I believe that our perspectives and paths are informed by our own individual collection of experiences. I recognize that I am who I am today because of the people and experiences throughout my life.

You'll notice that I specifically mentioned that employee ownership is my primary *professional* mission. While this is my professional mission, my highest mission is my family. I owe this ability to prioritize my highest mission while championing employee ownership to my wife, Mandy, who has always kept me grounded in what is most important. When work gets busy, she gives me the grace and support I need, but she's also right there to nudge me to shift my attention to our family, including our four kids and six grandkids, if I get too tunnel-visioned on work.

How I view the world was shaped at a young age by how my parents raised me and my siblings. The lessons and mindsets that they possessed and shared with us are ones that I still carry with me today and utilize in leading HB Global.

My mom has instilled in me the spirit of entrepreneurism. She was a beautician who owned her own salon in our house, serving women in the community for 25 years. As I was graduating college, she shifted her focus to cutting kids' hair. When she finished her days as a beautician, she started selling Jaguar cars. She had always loved Jaguars and decided to pivot her career in that direction. She then made another career shift and has been an interior decorator for the past 15 to 20 years, with no formal training. Not only did growing up watching my mom help me to embrace entrepreneurism, but I also admired her willingness to take risks and go different directions. The three stages of her career were vastly different from each other, but she excelled in each of them.

That willingness to take risks and dive into new ventures is how I ended up acquiring HB McClure. People thought I was nuts to buy a business in an industry I knew nothing about, but I had watched my mom be successful at this time and again. This continues to play out today in how we diversify our geography, industries, and business lines at HB Global.

My dad has taught me the value of hard work. He was a union electrician, and the most important thing to him was working hard. There was a discipline around hard work that showed up in everything he did. Let me tell you a story that will paint the picture for you.

When I was 18 years old, my parents were building a new house. At the time, my dad was working the night shift and then would come home and work on the house all day long. I very specifically remember when we put stone in the basement to serve as the base for the concrete. There was a huge pile of stone, and we were using wheelbarrows to get the stone down to the basement. I was 18 years old and an athlete; I was in great shape, and he still absolutely buried me at this activity... after working the night shift. And it was absolutely his intent to outwork me and show me what real hard work looked like.

My dad taught me that when it came time to work, you worked hard. While I believe in moderation of everything and striving for a solid integration of work and life whenever possible, I also know there are times when we have to put our heads down and get the work done, and I always have the discipline to do that when needed because of my dad.

I would also be remiss to not mention my grandfather. When I graduated from college, he sat me down and showed me a plan that he'd put together for me. It showed how if I saved a certain amount of every paycheck for my whole career that I could end up being a millionaire.

That started my interest in and passion for the power of compounding. I saw the importance of saving early and consistently. I now work to pass that knowledge on by demonstrating how savings through ESOP balances can grow and compound over a career, with the goal of our employees becoming millionaires.

While I learned so much from my parents, the last major mindset they instilled in me that I'll mention for the purposes of this book is how we view others. My parents were adamant that nobody was better than us and that nobody was less than us. That perspective helped me immensely early in my career, in that I took on new opportunities and interacted with high-level business folks without being intimidated. After all, we all put our pants on the same way every day.

This philosophy is also a major contributor to my passion for ESOPs. When we believe that nobody is any better than or any less than anyone else, we see how important it is for us to share the value that a company is producing with everyone who is responsible for producing that value. After all, we are all part of the same team, and each team member has an important role. To me, whether we share profit or not shouldn't be based on whether we went to graduate school or the school of hard knocks; each company needs both sets of team players. At HB Global, we need both MBAs and technical employees to be successful.

It's no different than a football team. Growing up, I played football. On a football team, you have two sides of the ball and 11 players on the field at a time for each side. Each of these roles is highly specialized, and a successful football team needs each of these roles. Each team member adds immense value because of that. Tom Brady is one of the greatest football players we've seen, but things probably wouldn't go so well for him if he tried to step in as an offensive lineman, nor would they go so well for him if he didn't have his tackles.

Football was actually the sport I loved the most, but unfortunately, I wasn't good enough to go play at the Division 1 level. I did, however, receive a Division 1 wrestling scholarship. My family needed me to take that scholarship to play my part. While there is a misconception that wrestling is largely an individual sport, it also fueled my passion for teamwork. To me, it was always the most important thing. People often wondered how I stayed so cool under pressure while I was out on the mat with so many eyes staring at me (wrestling is a big deal in Pennsylvania), and it was because I was more focused on the success of the team than my individual success. Of course, we wanted to win individual championships, but we were always focused on the team and would step into whatever role we needed to in order to ensure the team's success.

I earned my bachelor's degree in Agricultural Economics from Cornell University. I was fortunate to be able to see the concept of team in action at my first business experience out of college at Continental Medical. This early career experience is where I picked up the importance of integrating a company's mission, vision, and core values into everything it does. People were a priority for this company. I still carry that with me today as I strive to scale our culture and have our mission, vision, and core values be a guide for everything we do. It was such a great experience that I still have a mentor today from this company.

After Continental Medical, I joined Integrated Health Services. They stated that they wanted to be the employer of choice, but from where I stood, it never seemed that they thought of the employees at all when making decisions. Coming from Continental Medical, which was incredibly focused on building a strong culture and environment for employees, to working for a company that fell on the other end of the spectrum, my time there did not last long. While not necessarily related to the culture, it is worth noting that Integrated Health Services eventually went bankrupt.

When I left Integrated Health Services, I started my own boutique consulting firm called CBA Consulting. I served the employee benefits space. I eventually ended up selling my business to Mercer in 2003. I then held various positions with them for five years and pursued my Master of Business Administration (MBA) at Cornell, at which time I decided I wanted to run my own company.

I made a few other stops along the way throughout my career and later also earned my Master of Science in Finance (MSF) at Notre Dame. Overall, I ended up working for three different multinational companies with tens of thousands of employees. What I learned from those experiences was how out of touch really smart people at a centralized corporate organization can be with what's going on in the markets.

Not only is this not good for business, but it's demotivating to employees closest to the customers when a corporate employee removed from their day-to-day is making certain decisions for them. As I've grown in my career, I've also seen academic data support this.

Decision-making happening closest to the customers is especially important to me because my parents were blue-collar workers. I valued, and continue to value, those roles and how important they are to a company. Leadership tucked away in a centralized corporate structure can't always have a full view into what's happening in the field, but that is still crucially important to the success of the business.

I came out of college believing that maximizing shareholder value was the goal of a corporation, but my experiences have made that viewpoint more nuanced. I believe profit and capitalism are important, but I now believe in a more holistic view of that. While those factors are necessary for the success of the business, there also needs to be a focus on the employees, customers, and suppliers. When I got out of college and had the opportunity to see a people-focused business at Continental Medical, it made me start to wonder who we were maximizing shareholder value for. Who and what would benefit from that shareholder value?

There's a tendency to think that we need to be on one extreme or the other. In this case, those extremes could be maximizing short-term shareholder return at all costs on one end or ensuring that everyone is paid equally and has an equal say in a company on the other. I believe we can move towards the middle and incorporate both sides of the equation. It's important to have moderation in our lives, and business is no different. For example, we all know that sugar is bad for us, but it's also not realistic or sustainable to totally cut sugar out of our diets; we consume it in moderation. My view is the same on integrating work and life. Moderation is the key.

I also recognize that my way is not the only way. It fits my personality and belief system, and I believe that, if my way works, the results will speak for themselves. However, I don't begrudge others for feeling otherwise. That's something I'd like for you to remember throughout the book as you consider whether an ESOP is a good fit for you.

After my MBA, I knew I wanted to try my hand at testing all the beliefs and learnings that I'd acquired throughout my career by running my own company. I had grown up in the Harrisburg, PA area and had always seen the blue and yellow HB McClure service trucks driving around. They were a highly respected company in our area that I felt I would be lucky to run. When I heard that Bob McClure was looking to sell, I jumped at the opportunity to be able to continue the legacy of the blue and yellow while creating a positive impact on our community and growing the mark of the brand.

Then

Now

You know what happened after that, and I invite you to journey with me through the book to see how the ESOP has panned out since that fateful board meeting. I'm looking forward to sharing more personal stories, stories from our company, and stories of our employees with you throughout this book to exemplify the magic of ESOPs.

****

In this book, we'll cover various aspects of ESOPs, but let me first start by saying this is not a technical book. Rather, this book is designed to provide you with a high-level overview of what's possible in the world of ESOPs by using captivating real-world examples, especially from what I know best... our story at HB Global. This is intended to be a great introduction to the power of ESOPs, and I hope it can cultivate your interest before you move on to the technical details because – if I'm being honest – starting with those is often a turnoff. Any business will have complexities to work through, so before we worry about those, let's talk about the power of this structure. All that being said, I have included a list of some additional resources in the appendix. However, I always recommend consulting with an ESOP advisor and ESOP tax specialist as you move through the process. After all, I'm just the CEO of a mechanical contracting company who has found great success for both myself and our employees through the impact of an ESOP.

Each chapter will also end with me "On My Soapbox." While the entire book is, of course, written based on my knowledge, experiences, and beliefs, these sections are set apart intentionally. The topics included in these sections are ones that I am particularly passionate about but that others don't always see eye-to-eye with me on.

Between chapters, we've also included sections titled "Another Perspective," which showcase viewpoints on employee ownership from actual employee owners at HB Global or former business owners who sold their business to HB Global.

Okay, so we won't be diving into the technicalities of ESOPs. What will we be covering? In this book, I'd like to take you on a journey.

We're going to start with what sets this book apart. We're going to talk about how ESOPs and capitalism work together. I'm passionate about the ESOP structure because I think it's a great way to increase median income for the masses. Many will beat the drum for ESOPs as a way to redistribute wealth. In my opinion, that viewpoint is divisive. Instead, we can all have our cake and eat it, too. ESOPs receive bipartisan support for a reason; they support the American experiment.

We'll then talk briefly about what employee ownership is. This is a crash course in some of the most foundational high-level aspects that you'll want to know heading into the rest of the book. Then, we'll take an unexpected turn.

We'll get the elephant out of the room and talk about failure before we move any further into the book. When ESOPs first became a formalized business structure, there were many highly publicized failures. There have even been some recent stories that haven't painted ESOPs in the greatest light. We need to address this head-on. Generally speaking, ESOP companies don't fail because they are an ESOP; they fail because of a lack of sound business practices. A theme you will see throughout the book is that an ESOP is not a silver bullet for business. Running an ESOP still requires executing well on a business plan, making sound decisions, and fostering an aligned culture.

After we get that out of the way, we'll spend some time on practical and logistical topics. We'll get you thinking about what your intentions might be before transitioning your business and why it's important to think about those intentions early, not just when you approach retirement. I then may surprise you with what I want to spend time on next: alternative options for transitioning ownership of your business. Yes, I think ESOPs are the greatest thing since sliced bread, but it doesn't mean they are right for everyone. I don't want to force something this major on you; I'm here to create awareness, and part of that is letting you know your options.

As long as we're talking about options, we'll then move into a discussion on the flexibility of ESOPs. ESOPs aren't designed to be a one-size-fits-all structure. Chances are, you can find a way to set it up that aligns with your goals and priorities. This leads into how ESOPs can help create a win-win-win scenario. We'll wrap up by tangibly demonstrating how we win through ESOPs by discussing the alpha that can be created through this structure. (If you don't know what alpha is... hold tight, we'll discuss that).

We'll spend the last portion of the book discussing the emotional and cultural aspects of ESOPs. We'll start by talking broadly about the culture of employee ownership. This will lead us into discussions on the importance of employee engagement in an ESOP model and how ESOPs create a unity of purpose.

Before moving on, there's one important point I'd like to cover. When we communicate internally with our employees, we address them as "employee owners." They aren't just employees but are also owners in our company. Using the term "employee owners" throughout the book became a bit cumbersome, so for your ease of reading, we simply refer to employee owners at our ESOP (or other ESOPs) as employees throughout the book. The more you read, the more you will see how employees at an ESOP are inherently owners, so I didn't want you to have to stumble over words.

I'd like to thank you in advance for journeying through this book with me. I'm excited to illuminate the potential for you to align your purpose, people, and profits through the opportunities that ESOPs create for personal success, the success of your employees, the legacy of your business, the impact on your community, and the impact on generations to come. Let's dive in.

Chapter 1

The Role of Employee Ownership in Capitalism

I believe in capitalism. I believe capital providers should get a rate of return relative to the risk that they're taking, but I also believe that it benefits our society to recognize that the laborers working for our businesses are required for success. And why shouldn't they be compensated in some way for the value that they're adding to a business? The ESOP structure is a great way to do that.

ESOPs are often construed as a way to address wealth inequities. I think it's time to take a new approach to this outlook. We need to look at ESOPs as a collaborative effort and a self-reinforcing win for all, rather than an us-versus-them mentality of shifting wealth from the ownership class to the labor class.

The government also supports the role of ESOPs in a capitalist system. They do this by subsidizing the creation of employee-owned companies by giving those companies the advantage of not having to pay income tax.

At HB Global, we understand both sides of the coin and demonstrate how employee ownership not only fits into the capitalist structure but enhances it. We've participated in the capital markets by taking on senior debt and subordinate debt. In our case, the subordinate debt has come from the former owners of the businesses we've acquired. This subordinate debt has allowed us to take on more debt than what senior lenders would typically provide on their own, while allowing us increased flexibility. Those capital providers have then gotten a return on their investments. Textbook capitalism.

Our structure at HB Global is also set up so that 100% of the value our company creates is shared with the labor that produces it. There are no outside equity owners. The ESOP creates the mechanism to share that equity. (We'll talk later about the flexibility regarding how much of a company is considered an ESOP.)

So, HB Global takes on debt and repays those capital providers, invests capital into sustaining and growing our business, and our equity owners have been huge benefactors of our success. We are set up to succeed in a capitalist economy. The difference between us and the majority of US businesses is that 100% of the value we create is shared with the labor that produces it.

On the flip side, we've also created HB Capital outside of the HB Global ESOP, where we can be a capital provider. Companies generally need equity capital to start the process of becoming an ESOP; the risk to the company is far too high if they finance 100% of the transition with debt capital. Furthermore, senior and subordinate debt markets are not likely to provide everything the company needs. At HB Capital, we step in and acquire the company as a standard private equity vehicle. The main difference is that at the end of the typical three- to seven-year exit period, we exit the business to an ESOP. The same capital provider that benefited in the early stage can exit to a debt provider. The senior debt is paid off, and the subordinate debt is replaced with senior debt. An example is shown on the next page.

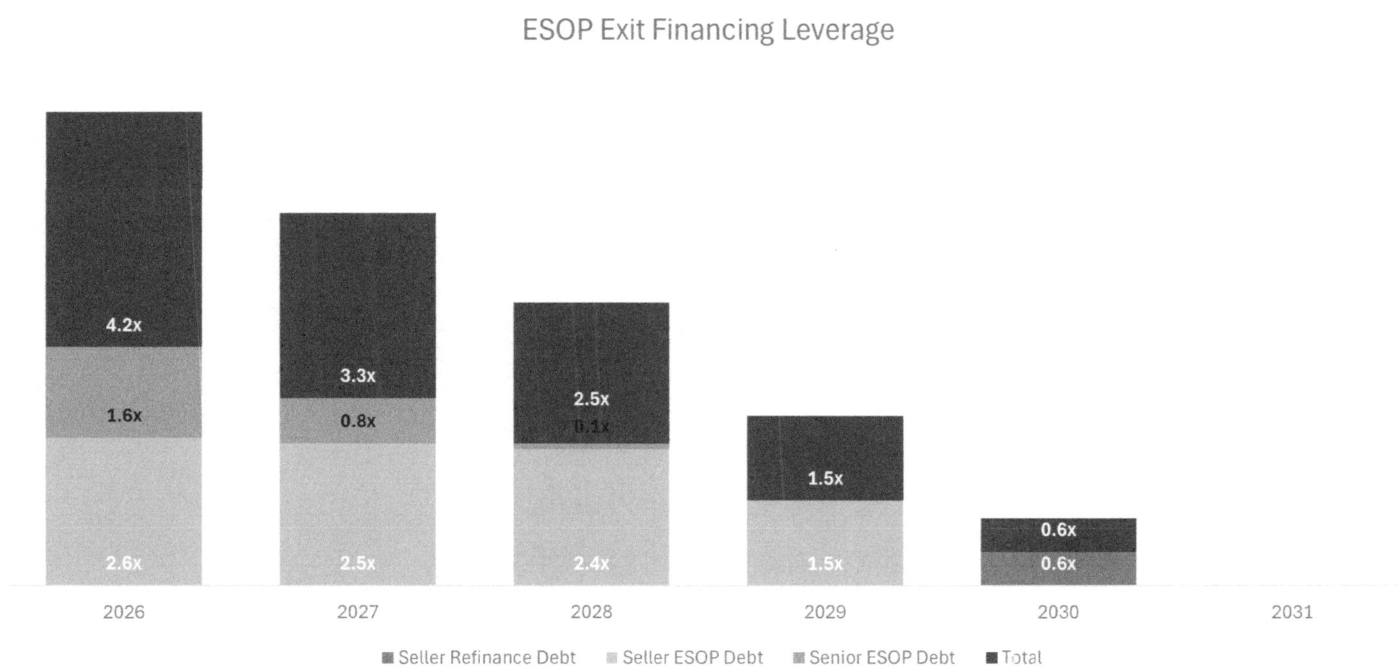
ESOP Exit Financing Leverage
4.2x
1.6x
2.6x
3.3x
0.8x
2.5x
2.5x
0.1x
2.4x
1.5x
1.5x
0.6x
0.6x
2026
2027
2028
2029
2030
2031
Seller Refinance Debt
Seller ESOP Debt
Senior ESOP Debt
Total

Because of these two facets of the HB brand, I can attest as a participant in capital markets and as a capital provider that employee ownership is not in opposition to capitalism. In fact, it's quite the opposite.

Capitalism and Employee Ownership

While it may seem obvious, let's start with the basics. An important part of a capitalist system is investing cash, and the people investing that cash should get a return to show for it. Otherwise, why would they put it at risk? I think most people would be aligned with that explanation of capitalism.

I would argue, however, that not only is capital important to the success of our economy but that labor should share in that success. An increase in outcomes for our labor would also likely lead to an increase in productivity within the economy.

We see this at technology companies all the time. Sure, the executives are highly compensated, but there's a large part of the employee base sharing in that success as well. As a recent example, a 2025 survey of Nvidia employees showed that approximately 50% of their employees had a net worth over $25 million, and about 80% of employees were millionaires![2] Why it doesn't get that much attention is because there's a large, high-paid workforce in those companies that benefited from the sharing in that success. That's not as great a story as a receptionist or a plumber becoming millionaires, but the fact of the matter is that some of these companies have made millionaires out of technical employees.

The idea of employee ownership is not a new one. But employee ownership can take place in a variety of ways, and what I'm advocating for is a commitment on the front end, before the resources are ever created,

[2] Ananya Gairola, "Nvidia Is Producing 'Unprecedented Wealth' For Its Employees, Nearly 80% Are Already Millionaires: Report," Yahoo!Finance, August 5, 2023, https://finance.yahoo.com/news/nvidia-producing-unprecedented-wealth-employees-003124691.html?guccounter=1&guce_referrer=aHR0cHM6Ly9kb2NzLmdvb2dsZS5jb20v&guce_referrer_sig=AQAAAJ669HPD_GO2TVJ87SsAUe11ZhkzJfpVY1k5iC8SeVTSSjrJUrAI5D5ckvYYJaghOx8zLLILwmFdjZIjRN632CXUGMfL3YScaalH-cRRJY89olo9l9G-goxNfTyVQ5X7qh6VbeSuiVSLWCxaRhGv0o77nqlVY8_LA17WMvZQ11og.

to support the labor that is crucial to the success of the company. Then, the wealth created after the commitment is shared with the labor and capital providers. This view says that the company is committing to employees having a stake in the business and being tied to its success.

In 2022, there were approximately 6,500 ESOPs.[3] I would argue that if we had more broad based employee ownership, not only would productivity increase but the resulting wealth on a large scale would increase as well. In other words, it doesn't just reallocate the wealth pie when done right, but instead it increases the size of the pie while ensuring that the success of companies is more fairly shared. It means median income should increase with the wider adoption of employee ownership.

The potential of ESOPs to revolutionize capitalism while staying true to the fundamental elements of it is so great that there are even tax incentives for companies that structure themselves this way.

Employee ownership is exemplary of capitalism because capital providers, largely through debt markets, are still getting a return on their investment, and equity owners are still sharing in the wealth on an ongoing basis. In this structure, however, the equity owners are the employees of the company. Capital providers still thrive, and employees now thrive as well, while having a say in the outcomes at their place of work.

In an ESOP structure, all the constituencies are working together to make the company successful. This doesn't just mean employees being aligned because they get to share in the success of the company, but it also means that leadership is keeping the best interests of the employees in mind. Employees generally come into a company with cynicism towards the management, executive, and ownership class. While an ESOP definitely helps to alleviate this cynicism, conscientious effort still needs to be put in to ensure that there is alignment and buy-in that everyone in the company has each other's best interests in mind and are sharing in the success of the company.

[3] "Employee Ownership by the Numbers," National Center for Employee Ownership, nceo.org, updated February 2025, https://www.nceo.org/research/employee-ownership-by-the-numbers#how-many-esops-are-there.

An ESOP structure still allows for the "natural selection" of capitalism to take place. Any of the same pitfalls that would apply to any other business still apply to ESOPs. Part of capitalism is that there is an efficient deployment of resources. Labor is deployed when there's a rate of return. Sure, there are some short-sighted labor decisions that are still made in a capitalist system, but in general, part of why capitalism works is that we don't make too many horseshoes and buggies when we don't need them anymore.

How Employee Ownership Benefits Society as a Whole

ESOPs don't just benefit businesses and employees in a capitalist economy, they also benefit society as a whole. We'll talk more about this later in the book, but the most obvious benefit is that when a company uses its profits to support its employees' retirement, those employees require less support from the government later on. In theory, this results in the working class paying less taxes, which means more take home pay.

While that is just a theory and politics are unpredictable, ESOPs benefit communities in a very real way in the here and now. Let's consider the difference between a private equity firm buying a business as compared to the business transitioning to an ESOP. If the business becomes an ESOP, a large part of the financial returns and success of that company stay in the community. Profits are shared with employees, which then benefits their families, other local businesses, and more. Profits that are kept in the business are truly reinvested for the future growth of the business and long-term benefit of the employees. When a private equity firm buys a company, much of the financial gain is plucked out of the community and funneled to the financial centers these firms reside in, such as New York, Chicago, and Los Angeles. There is nothing fundamentally wrong with this. Private equity has its place, too, but the outcomes will look different. While the concept of Americans retiring to Florida or Arizona has been romanticized, most working-class Americans retire where they are.

When financial returns are pulled out of the communities where a company is located and funneled to financial centers, typically the rich get richer, and the individuals in smaller suburban or rural areas are drained of resources. ESOPs create opportunities for reinvestment in the communities they serve. Not only do these ESOP companies provide goods and services, but they also provide steady jobs, compensation, and savings for the folks in those communities. According to Form 5500 data from filing year 2013, 54% of ESOP plans have been around for at least 20 years.[4] Furthermore, a study that tracked companies over 10 years found that privately held firms that were not employee-owned were twice as likely to go out of business as those that were employee-owned.[5] This holds true even in tough economic times. Fidan Ana Kurtulus and Douglas Kruse analyzed publicly traded companies from 1999 to 2011. In their study, the data showed that when the macroeconomic unemployment rate increased by one percentage point, firms without any employee ownership decreased their workforce by 3%, and ESOPs only decreased their workforce by 1.7%.[6]

I'm not naive. I know there are people who will still prefer to take as big a piece of the pie as they can and will justify it with valid reasons of their own. My goal isn't to force the ESOP structure on anyone. The freedoms of America are what make us the innovative and entrepreneurial country that we are.

The business owners who will likely be interested in ESOPs are those who have already been successful and have the legacy of their business and employees in mind. These owners want, and need, to get the liquidity out of their business but have a choice of how those resources are distributed in the future. Instead of a hollow victory when they exit, where they take their piece of the pie and leave the business and employees to fend for themselves, business owners who exit to an ESOP can exit with a legacy intact and their community of employees taken care of.

[4] "Economic Growth Through Employee Ownership" (PDF), National Center for Employee Ownership, nceo.org, accessed October 31, 2025, https://www.nceo.org/hubfs/assets/pdf/Economic_Growth_Through_EO.pdf.

[5] Corey Rosen and John Case, *Ownership: Reinventing Companies, Capitalism, and Who Owns What* (Berrett-Koehler Publishers, 2022): 85.

[6] Rosen and Case, *Ownership*: 119.

This vision will appeal to business owners who believe that "a rising tide raises all boats." In this case, the rising tide is what an ESOP creates, which is a great solution for owners who feel that sharing in success is a priority. While these owners are focused on the legacy of their business and the well-being of their employees, they're still able to get the liquidity they need out of the company as well. When I set out to acquire HB McClure, I had set financial goals for later in life and my retirement. Even though I've ended up sharing the pie with all employee owners at HB Global, I've still far exceeded the financial goals I was striving for.

An Updated Mindset

It's important to shift the mindset around employee ownership, and the shift I'm advocating for is nuanced. In my view, it's important to focus on improving the financial lives of employees rather than focus on shifting resources to solve wealth inequity.

"If the difference in mindset is nuanced, why worry about it?" you may be asking.

Oftentimes, the wealth inequity argument is used as a guilt mechanism. To me, it doesn't make sense to demonize those who have been most successful in the system, which is where the argument of solving the wealth inequity often heads. To make our society better, I don't think we should focus on how successful the most successful are, but rather, we should focus on improving where the bulk of our society is. One of my favorite books is *Enlightenment Now*. In that book, Steven Pinker makes the argument that, as a society, we keep on getting better and better – more free, more peaceful – but that all that gets lost in the noise of the day. I don't think we see this sort of progress when we alienate some of our highly productive members. We don't have to tear down the people who have been most successful because, without those most successful people, we would have lost a lot of productivity and innovation. Instead, we should take an approach that encourages aligned action.

Oftentimes, in society today, our workforce feels they're being exploited by the ownership class, and the ownership class feels they're being taken advantage of by the working class. This creates two juggernaut sides fighting against each other philosophically about how wealth is distributed.

Our tax system is a great depiction of this concept. There's a general belief within the United States that those with a lot of wealth have not paid their fair share in taxes. Generally speaking, society has gone on the attack. This puts those with wealth on the defensive when others feel they aren't contributing sufficiently to society. The fact is that those with the most wealth are pulling their weight. In 2021, the top 1% paid 45.8% of all the income taxes that were paid. The top 5% of earners paid 65.6%, and the top 10% paid 75.8%. The top 50% of earners paid 97.7% of all income taxes for the year.[7] The top earners are pulling their weight in taxes.

Shifting our mindset to one where we create a team approach across the board and embrace what those with wealth have done can lead to greater outcomes. Yes, it may yield a result in which labor gets a bigger piece of the existing pie, but through alignment of action, we're actually likely to increase the size of the pie that is shared. I don't think we make progress in this effort by attacking a group that can help.

I'm fighting for a world where we create an environment in which we're aligned with a shared goal. Not only do businesses and employees benefit from that, but customers and communities benefit as well from the productivity of the business and the success of those in the community. The cycle becomes self-reinforcing and helps to grow the wealth pie.

This entrepreneurial spirit is rooted in how the US was formed. We are a country founded with freedoms and independence in mind. Because of that, we've attracted many individualists. I would put myself in this category. I don't respond well when I'm told I "have to" do something, and I think that's true with most of our population. Trying to solve wealth inequity purely from a redistribution mindset approaches the argument through a negative mechanism and is rampant with "have to's." Trying to increase the size of the pie by putting our arms around the ownership and executive class and approaching the issue as a team is a positive mechanism that can make real progress.

[7] USAFacts team, "Who pays the most income tax?" USA Facts, usafacts.org, updated June 25, 2025, https://usafacts.org/articles/who-pays-the-most-income-tax/.

ESOPs aren't the only way to approach this issue. There are plenty of successful family businesses that share the wealth that they generate. I'm not saying the ESOP is the only way. But I am passionate about ESOPs because they are a systematic way with bipartisan support that is incentivized by the government for the working class and the ownership class to come together and work towards increasing the pie. No one wants to run a company where they are at war with their employees the whole time. ESOPs are a systematic way to get everyone on the same team and be transparent about the wealth being created and how it's being distributed.

On My Soapbox – Freedom of Choice

In order for us to have the freedom to thrive, we can't eliminate the freedom to fail. I believe that part of our freedom in the United States is that we also have the choice to do things that don't lead us to success. We can't have freedom in only one direction where freedom only leads to the upside. Of course, we as a society don't specifically do things in anticipation that they'll lead to failure, but there are some pretty concrete examples that we can point to.

Let's look at healthcare as an example. We often want to examine our healthcare outcomes in the US compared to those in Europe. This analysis is typically done in the debate as to what the healthcare system in the US should look like. But it's not enough to just look at the outcomes, because this issue conflates a variety of factors, one of those being our freedom to fail. We can make the choice to smoke, have a high sugar intake, drink alcohol, eat fast food every day, not look before we cross the road, and a whole host of other choices. None of those decisions typically lead to positive health outcomes and are not a result of our healthcare system. Instead, they're a result of the freedoms we have. I don't think anyone reading this book wants their right to have a drink on a Friday night or to smoke a cigar to celebrate a special occasion taken away.

Not only would taking away these choices rub us the wrong way as individualistic citizens, but it would also take away innovative freedom. My view is that we should put our arm around the people with the most resources and try to work with them instead of demonizing them.

I don't think someone like Bill Gates would want to be seen as not pulling his weight for society. Bill Gates, Warren Buffett, and a whole host of other people with resources maintain their freedom to address problems that are most important to them.

As a business owner, you have the freedom to make a choice to benefit the employees who helped you build or grow your business as you consider your legacy upon exit. There's a way for you to exit your company comfortably and positively impact your business, community, and society as a whole.

If you're tired and just want to exit quickly and sell to private equity or a strategic buyer, and trust your business to another owner, that is your prerogative. It may be a good fit for you depending on your priorities. I'm arguing that there's a different way. By choosing to form an ESOP, you can have the value you create stay in your communities and help people whose names and faces you actually know.

As part of this freedom to choose, you can choose to be part of the solution rather than focusing on the divide. I don't begrudge people making other choices, but I believe the choice to structure a business as an ESOP is not widely known, and one of my missions is to make this choice more widely known, using the success of our company as an example of the positive impact it can make for all.

Another Perspective – Bob McClure and Andy Henry

Let's hear from Bob McClure for his perspective on selling his company, HB McClure, to Bob Whalen and converting it to an ESOP.

1. *What were your priorities when selling your company?*

> That the company would continue and thrive, and the employees that helped us be successful would be rewarded and able to continue their careers.
>
> And that I would be able to live the rest of my life as I had grown accustomed to.

2. *How did it feel selling your company to an ESOP?*

> The ESOP option was the only way for my answers for the first question to be achieved.

3. *How would you describe the success and legacy of your business today?*

> Incredible, and way beyond my wildest hopes and dreams! And Bob Whalen is my hero!

Let's hear from Andy Henry, who was the CFO at HB McClure when it was converted to an ESOP in 2010.

1. *What were your priorities when selling your company?*

> The initial priority was for all existing employees to retain their jobs with little if any change in operations and that nobody lost their job simply because of the sale.
>
> Another priority was for the key leadership employees to be heavily engaged in contributing

towards a controlled and systematic change of ownership.

Retaining the long-standing culture created by several generations of family ownership was a priority as well.

2. *How did it feel selling your company to an ESOP?*

Being personally involved in the original sale of the Company and involved in the subsequent ESOP conversion a few years later, I knew it had the potential to be a huge financial benefit to every single employee, but not without its risks. Once I had a solid understanding of our ESOP blueprint and I became more knowledgeable on ESOPs in general, I knew we stood a very good chance of being a successful ESOP. Little did I know just how successful our ESOP would turn out to be to this very day.

3. *How would you describe the success and legacy of your business today?*

The success and legacy of our business today is nothing short of astonishing. We have been wildly successful in our ESOP goals for the employee owners (share price growth) and for the Company's financial success and growth. We have maintained our priorities established during the sale of our Company, which were incorporated into our mission statement long ago. The sale of the Company and subsequent ESOP sale all focused on the employee and their success. Their success created a dedicated and appreciative client base that has created our ongoing financial successes. It's important to understand that exceptional success comes from exceptional leadership. We have exceptional leadership.

Being with our Company for 42 years gives me more insight than most on our legacy. The Company's legacy is something very few companies have or will have achieved. From a less than a million-dollar revenue Company to over half a billion, from less than 100 employees to over a thousand, from family-owned to employee-owned, with growing ESOP accounts valued at over a million dollars. All this while our CEO, who bought the Company in 2008 and turned it ESOP in 2010, maintains the one fundamental priority that existed back in the 1980s; take care of our employees. Owners looking to sell and have a desire to see their businesses and employees thrive long after their time need to consider the advantages of an ESOP.

Chapter 2
What Does Employee Ownership Mean?

We transitioned to an ESOP by selling HB McClure to an ESOP trust in 2010. At that time, there were 133 employees eligible to participate in the ESOP. Of those 133 employees, 61 are still employed today (2024). While that in itself is a testament to the culture that an ESOP helps facilitate by putting a focus on employee owners, the numbers round out the story.

When those employees were allocated shares the first year we became an ESOP, the allocation they received was worth just $600 (which they couldn't even access until retirement). For those 61 employees who have been with us for the last 14 years, the median balance in their ESOP retirement accounts is now $392,000 (as of the 2023/2024 plan year)! And these impressive balances will continue to grow and compound from here on out.

> **Technical note:** The term "allocation" is used when shares are placed in employees' ESOP accounts. The term "distribution" is used when former employees are paid cash in exchange for those shares after they leave the company or retire.

A study by the National Center for Employee Ownership from January 2022 showed that the average ESOP account balance was $132,362, while the average 401(k) balance for companies that only offered this retirement savings vehicle was $63,925. Outside of retirement savings, studies have also shown that employees working at employee-owned companies earn 5% to 12% more than employees at comparable non-ESOP companies.[8]

What Is an ESOP?

An ESOP is an Employee Stock Ownership Plan. In its most simplistic form, employee ownership means that, as an employee, you're an owner of the business that you work for. What being an owner means is that, for whatever percentage of the business you own, you are entitled to that same percentage of resources created by that business.

An ESOP is essentially an employer-funded retirement plan. Because it is employer-funded, there is no contribution required, or even allowed, by the employee into the plan. This retirement plan owns equity in the company that established it.

One big incentive for companies to be structured this way is that ESOPs of S Corporations don't have to pay an income tax for the percentage owned by the ESOP. Instead, the taxes are deferred until the shareholders (employee owners) pay taxes on what they are paid for their ownership in the company at retirement. The tax efficiency

[8] Rosen and Case, *Ownership*: 86.

comes into play because shareholders (employee owners) are taxed at their own individual tax brackets, not at company tax rates, which is oftentimes a higher rate than the individual rate.

> **Technical Note:** Employees aren't actually individual shareholders of the company. There's a trust that is technically the shareholder, and the employees get the financial benefit of those shares. For more information on the technicalities of an ESOP structure, please consult professionals in this field. You can also find additional educational resources in the appendix.

For those of you who may be skeptical that this just allows the company to push the tax burden onto employees, consider this: Because the company is not subject to income taxes, more of the profit that is generated is shared back to employees, leading to more money in their pockets.

Another big advantage to the ESOP structure is that, because it's a retirement plan, employees benefit from the tax deferred compounding of financial resources over the time period that they're with the company and until the resources are distributed to the employee. There is a significant opportunity for compounding (which we'll talk more about later in the chapter) because the employee doesn't have access to that cash in their account in any way until it is distributed.

Compared to ESOP programs, a more common way typical American companies help employees save for retirement is through a 401(k) retirement fund. In a 401(k), employees are able to take loans out or make hardship withdrawals, which are not available in an ESOP. However, most 401(k) plans will require some sort of contribution on the part of the employee. Employers may decide to match the employee's contribution up to a certain percentage, but that is often dependent on the employee first making a contribution.

As I'll demonstrate throughout the book, ESOPs are incredibly flexible; here's our first example of that. ESOPs are not required to contribute to 401(k) plans. In fact, when we created the ESOP, we actually stopped our 401(k) match program to save on expenses during the Great Recession. If an ESOP company isn't providing a 401(k) match, employees still have the ability to make their own 401(k) contributions.

If an ESOP has an appetite to also set up a 401(k) match for their employees, they have the freedom to do that. In 2024, we began offering a 401(k) employer contribution in addition to the ESOP contributions that employees receive. Our 401(k) contribution is set up as a grant so employees receive contributions to their 401(k)s even if they don't contribute themselves, and they still receive the ability to take loans out against this account or make hardship withdrawals.

There are pros and cons to both the ESOP and the 401(k), however, I believe the fact that the cash in each ESOP account cannot be accessed until distribution creates great compounding opportunities and helps protect the longer-term resources of the employee. We'll talk more about this later in the chapter.

What Does Employee Ownership Mean to Employees?

It's no surprise that creating an employee-owned company hugely impacts employees. Some benefits are obvious and some are less obvious. There are two main aspects to it. There's a psychological component of the fulfillment and pride that comes with having an ownership stake in the business they work for, and there's the very real and tangible aspect of the financial resources created and shared on their behalf as owners of the company.

The tricky part is that employees believe they're actually owners of the company at different speeds. This is important because the maximum benefit is created for an ESOP company when all employees have bought in. So if 30% of the employees have bought in, you're creating more benefit than if no employees have bought in. However, if only 30% of employees buy in, you're not reaching the full potential that you would if everyone committed to this concept. While it's improbable to have 100% buy-in, companies can strive for a strong majority to generate as much value as possible.

Ultimately, employees benefit from their own actions. How employees are viewed by their supervisors and leadership is positively impacted when they buy in. This is easy to see because employees who have fully bought in are making every effort they can to generate value for the company. Employee buy-in benefits the individual employee and the company as a whole.

There are early adopters of employee ownership who think it's the best thing ever on Day 1. They realize the benefits they'll receive, and they're all in without you hardly having to explain why employee ownership is so great for them.

For most employees, the adoption increases as there's more money in their accounts. We saw this in the early years. As employees started to see more financial resources in their accounts, they began to make the connection between their own accounts and the performance of the company. At this point, the realization began to hit that their work was meaningful in driving the financial performance of the company, which would drive their own financial success.

The most enlightened employees realize that their efforts are actually not only benefiting them but are helping their co-workers who are also owners getting value shared back to them as a result of the success of the company. These people realize that they are a critical component to their teammates' success and that their teammates are critical to their own success. As this realization sinks in, self-accountability increases over time.

As the belief in employee ownership increases, the culture is directly impacted as well. Employees are more fulfilled by their work when they see that they benefit from the success of the company.

Oftentimes, workers become disenchanted with the typical business world as they move through their formative working years and fall victim to the negative connotation of working for someone else. They often feel that they're working to provide a certain lifestyle for those at the top.

In an ESOP, this nuance is taken away because employees can see that the work they are doing is coming back to benefit them. Working for an employee-owned company gives workers an opportunity to see financial benefits from the success of the company while getting to work in an established company with more resources than they themselves would have as an individual.

The business they work in can create more value as a whole company than they could as a sole proprietor. Employee owners of an ESOP company have access to the capital of the entire business that would not exist if they were operating as the owner of their own one-person business.

At HB Global, we've used over $200 million of outside capital. If you divide that amount by the number of employees at our company (~1,700 at the time of writing), that equates to $117,000 that each employee would have to come up with themselves, which exceeds the amount that many of them would have access to at any given moment on their own.

Let's give an example to show where the rubber meets the road. In 2021, HB Global acquired The Bell Company. At the time, we had about 1,500 employees. That means each employee owner would have had to come up with tens of thousands of dollars to make that acquisition. Instead, the company was able to finance the acquisition to create more value for the employees. And that's just one example. We've done over 25 acquisitions at this point where we go out and get the capital to make it happen, while the employees benefit from the value created from the growth of the company. My view is that it's our company's job to collect capital for growth, while our business and the employees within it create capital that generates value for the company and themselves.

There are, however, tricky parts to the psychology of employees. As employees within the company begin to buy in to the fact that they're an owner too, they start to treat the resources of the company as their own. This can be a pro and a con. It could lead to more responsible resource consumption or it could lead to some potentially poor decisions being made.

For example, technical employees may mistake the value of their time. They may spend an extra 30 minutes on a task to save $5 of materials when that 30 minutes of time was actually worth $25. This is a poor decision coming from an employee viewing company money in the same way they view their own money.

The executive class is not exempt from this either. They may have no expertise on a particular subject but want to be involved in a particular process or project because that process or project affects the value generated for the company. Ultimately, this can hinder the process or project.

Employees also become more invested not only in the decisions they're making but also in the decisions that others are making. For example, when I go to a business conference in Hawaii, I get questions because employees feel it's happening on their dime. When employees are working for someone else and don't share an ownership stake, the mentality is different.

We'll talk more about the cultural impacts of being an employee-owned company later in the book. For now, it's just important to know the immensely positive impact that this structure has on employees and that this effect is both financial and psychological in nature.

Leadership at Every Level

Employee ownership creates a culture based on everyone sharing in what's created. In this culture, employees have a tendency to engage in what the entity becomes and have agency around making that happen. This is a definite contrast to the traditional model in which employees are subservient to a leader who is driving the entire company.

At this point in the book, you might have some apprehension around the concept of the agency of employees. That's understandable. But employees having agency doesn't mean there's anarchy. It means that the entire group is working together towards the common good of the company. It means employees have the relevant information and tools to make decisions in the best interest of the organization. And it means people take accountability for their work because they had a role in finding the solution.

Employee agency doesn't mean there are no hierarchies or that leadership doesn't have a role. It just means that the role of leadership isn't overemphasized, and the individuals have more of a role in the impact they can make on the organization. Leadership and structure are important, but of equal importance is the ability of each individual employee.

Agency works because I've found that the more you allow people to find solutions, the more they take responsibility for the work they do. The opposite is true as well. The more you micromanage, the more employees shirk responsibility. The more I take control as a single leader, the more responsibility I take off of everyone else. But when I trust in the abilities of our employees to get the work done efficiently and effectively, a lot more gets accomplished, and everyone feels more fulfilled.

At HB Global, we have about 1,700 employees across the country. We do have a hierarchical structure and different levels of leadership roles. For us, agency means providing autonomy to those closest to the work being completed and giving employees the autonomy to take on things that are appropriate for their role and scope. Leaders are responsible for what they delegate to their teams and for holding their teams accountable for the results. This cascades autonomy and growth opportunities throughout the company.

Agency is a big component of the culture of employee ownership, as we'll talk about throughout the book, but it's not something that flips the company on its head and creates an every-person-for-themselves chaos.

The Power of Compounding

Because employee owners don't have access to cash from their ESOP accounts until the account is distributed, there is immense opportunity for the balance to benefit from the power of compounding, especially the longer the employee stays with the company.

In its simplest form, compounding basically means that the longer you invest in something, the more it's worth in the end. Let's take a look at a more detailed definition. According to Investopedia, "Compounding is the process in which an asset's earnings, from either capital gains or interest, are reinvested to generate additional earnings over time. This growth, calculated using exponential functions, occurs because the investment will generate earnings from both its initial principal and the accumulated earnings from preceding periods."[9]

Based on this definition, you can see that over time, you're receiving earnings not just on what's being invested but also on the balances that are already there, which includes the benefit of previous compounding. This adds up exponentially over time.

The following example calculations done by Mass Mutual demonstrate the impact of allowing compounding to happen over time. For example, if an individual starts saving $500 per month at age 22 with an 8% annual return, they will have $2,255,844 in savings by age 65 (before taxes and inflation). If an individual starts saving $500 a month at age 32 with an 8% annual return, they will instead have $972,542 at age 65 (before taxes and inflation). Waiting until age 42 to save in the same way leads to savings of $395,866 at age 65 before taxes and inflation.[10]

You can see how savings increase exponentially over time and how a few years can make a big difference in the grand scheme of saving. Playing the long game has immense benefits.

Unfortunately, we're our own worst enemies when it comes to compounding. We often don't stay disciplined as it relates to keeping our money in the accounts that will allow them to reap the full benefits of compounding and grow over the long term. It's human nature that we are subject to psychological factors as well, and I am not immune to this.

[9] James Chen, "Compounding Interest: Formulas and Examples," Investopedia, updated June 2, 2025, https://www.investopedia.com/terms/c/compounding.asp.

[10] Amy Fontinelle, "Saving for retirement in your 20s: Doing the math," Mass Mutual, blog.massmutual.com, February 6, 2025, https://blog.massmutual.com/retiring-investing/saving-retirement-20s.

My Blunder

Back in 2009, when my resources were depressed because of the recession, I allowed a financial advisor to talk me into investing in an annuity, rather than keeping my money in the stock market. This annuity guaranteed a 6% return and the markets historically returned 10%, but they were down, and I took the bait.

Despite having an MBA and robust financial knowledge, I still didn't exercise the discipline to keep my money in the typical indices and ride out the financial wave.

Hindsight is 20/20, and I now view this investment as a bond. But let me show you what would've happened if I had kept that chunk of money in the normal stocks I invest in rather than putting it in an annuity.

In the chart on the next page, we'll use a $1,000 investment as an example with a base year of 2008. You can see over time the slow, steady growth of the annuity as compared to how that same amount of money would have grown over that same time frame if it had been invested in the S&P 500.

Discipline from an ESOP

The great thing about an ESOP is that employees don't have a choice about removing their money from their accounts to make mistakes like me. Other than having opportunities to begin diversifying out of a portion of your employer securities at age 55 and after you have been in the plan for 10 years (whichever one comes last), the balance cannot be touched until it is distributed at retirement.[11]

This helps us to stay disciplined in our investing, rather than falling victim to circumstances that may cause us to panic, pull our money,

[11] "When Will I Be Paid? The ESOP Participant's Guide to ESOP Distribution Rules," National Center for Employee Ownership, nceo.org, accessed October 31, 2025, https://www.nceo.org/articles/how-esop-distributions-work-for-esop-participants-rules-and-guidance#:~:text=As%20an%20ESOP%20participant%2C%20you,you%20to%20direct%20its%20investment.

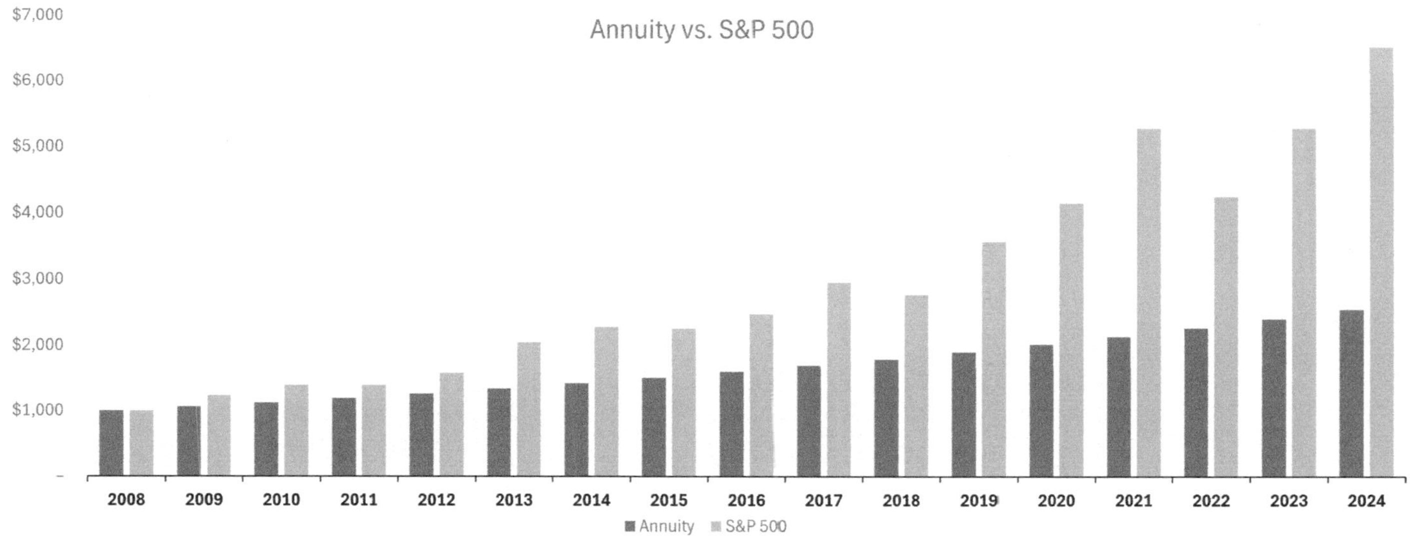
Annuity vs. S&P 500
$7,000
$6,000
$5,000
$4,000
$3,000
$2,000
$1,000
-
2008
2009
2010
2011
2012
2013
2014
2015
2016
2017
2018
2019
2020
2021
2022
2023
2024
Annuity
S&P 500

and spend it in the short-term or invest it elsewhere. As we've demonstrated, this compounding effect becomes more powerful over time. At BBEC, our subsidiary that started as an ESOP in 2000, multiple employee owners who have been with the company for the long term have account balances near or over one million dollars!

There is also power in the fact that an ESOP company is automatically contributing to your account – which then tracks with the performance of the company – as compared to employees at non-ESOP companies that typically need to invest in their own 401(k) and sometimes receive a match. On the next page, you can see the trajectory of a typical, median employee who started at HB Global in 2010, was still with us in 2024, and has $392,000 in their ESOP account. You'll see as a point of comparison the amount that an employee at a non-ESOP company would've had to save in order to match that. This example assumes a starting wage of $55,000 in 2010 with a 3% annual wage increase. This chart shows that in order for a comparable employee at a non-ESOP company to achieve a balance of $392,000 in their 401(k) account, they would have to contribute approximately $150,000 over the same 14-year period, which is a continuous contribution of almost 16% of their pay per year! It's important to recognize as well that the resulting balances are a combination of contributions to these accounts and return. For the ESOP account, the employer is making the contribution. For the 401(k), the employee is making the contribution.

For the 401(k) comparison, we are assuming the contributions are invested in the S&P 500, and we use the actual compound annual growth rate (CAGR) of the S&P 500 over that time period, which is 14.75%. This is important because the S&P 500 performance has generally been outstanding over that time period. With compounding, even a few percentage points of performance can make a significant difference. This demonstrates how much needs to be saved even during the fantastic performance of an index.

On My Soapbox – It's the Employer's Responsibility

Most of my friends think I'm nuts for this soapbox, but I'm pretty passionate about this one.

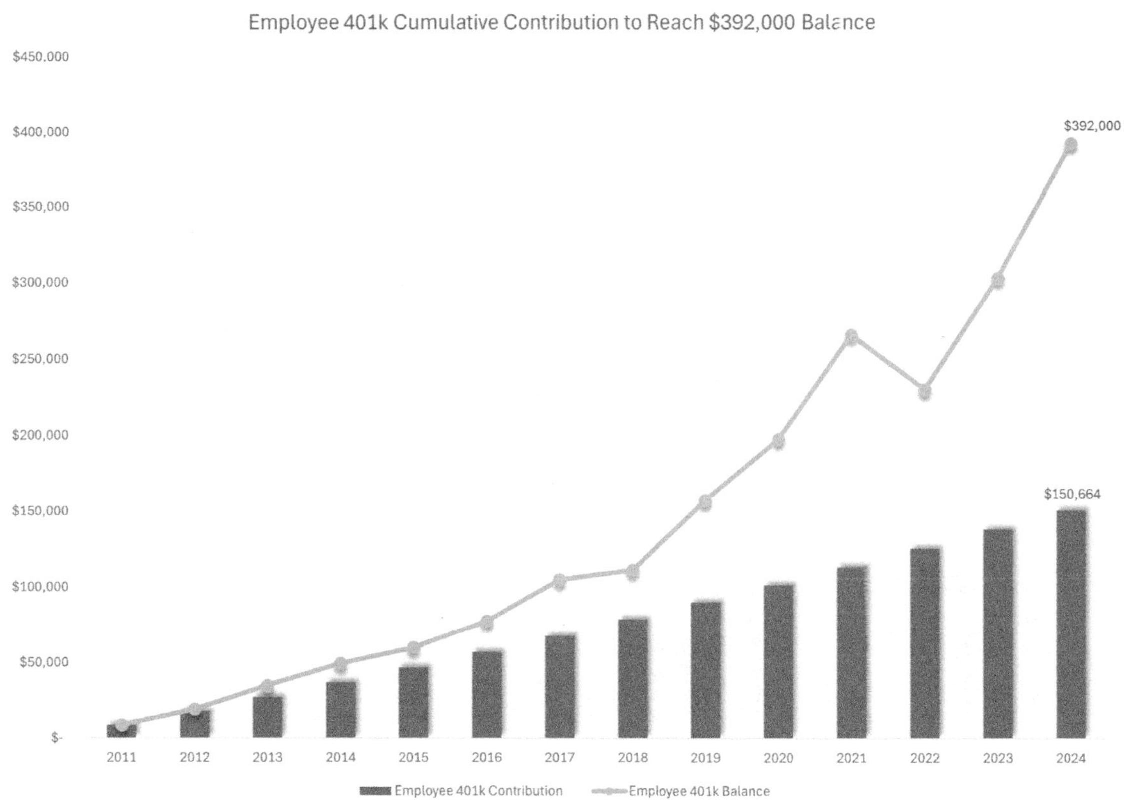
Employee 401k Cumulative Contribution to Reach $392,000 Balance
$450,000
$400,000
$350,000
$300,000
$250,000
$200,000
$150,000
$100,000
$50,000
$-
$392,000
$150,664
2011
2012
2013
2014
2015
2016
2017
2018
2019
2020
2021
2022
2023
2024
Employee 401k Contribution
Employee 401k Balance

We know that there are a lot of companies out there that, in essence, make it the employees' responsibility to save for their own retirement. The good ones give them the opportunity to do it with a 401(k) plan, 457, or whatever options they have, and a lot of them even support it with a match of the contribution that an employee puts in.

However, these types of plans most often require the primary contribution to come from the employee, and based on human behavior and statistical evidence, a large percentage of people will not do that when left to their own devices. In fact, according to USA Facts and the Federal Reserve's Survey of Consumer Finances, only 46% of households had *any* savings for retirement. 26% of households had saved over $100,000, and 9% of households had saved over $500,000.

While these statistics cover ages 18 – 94, the situation doesn't improve much as people near retirement age. For individuals 50 – 54 years old, only 63% had any savings for retirement, and only 35% of households had over $100,000 in savings for their retirement. To make matters worse, we know that a lot of compounding power is lost when saving starts later in life (although saving late is always better than never saving). This study also states that households with higher incomes are also the ones saving more for retirement.[12] As you'll see, this exacerbates the issue at hand.

I believe in our environment that it's the employer's responsibility to make sure that the employees end up with sufficient resources in retirement. It's my philosophy because it's just too big of an issue, based on the statistics we've seen, to not mitigate the risk that a certain percentage of people don't set aside sufficient savings for retirement.

It's not without precedent to do this type of thing. If we want to drive a vehicle, we are required to have car insurance. If this weren't a requirement, a number of people wouldn't do it because of the cost. Without insurance, society is burdened with those costs in the end, in one way or another. We don't make people have health insurance, and society is burdened with those costs in some way. An example of this is the charity care we provide in hospitals. This care is in essence built into

[12] USAFacts team, "Nearly half of American households have no retirement savings," USA Facts, usafacts.org, updated November 9, 2023, https://usafacts.org/data-projects/retirement-savings.

the charges that go to paying customers through either the individual paying those charges or through employer plans that are covering these costs. The hospital still gets reimbursed for those costs.

Philosophically, I believe that the basis for saving for retirement should be done through the employer. And instead of standing on my soapbox and saying we should do that and then not doing anything about it, we structured our company in a way to ensure that happened.

As a capitalist, I realize there are many objections to this philosophy. The first one is that people have a personal responsibility for their own obligations, which I'm generally all for. However, the reality is that a certain percentage of people will not exercise that personal responsibility of saving for their retirement.

Another common objection that I get is actually from the employee perspective. The counterargument here is that employees would prefer to put those resources to use in a different way, to be paid in the short-term. For example, they may want to use the resources to pay for braces, Little League baseball, etc. As a father, I understand the legitimacy of all those things. The reality is, however, that when we use those resources now, we don't save them for retirement.

While I'm all for personal responsibility and a capitalist who supports free markets and spending, the reality is this: we as a society will not tolerate not letting people have healthcare, food, housing, etc. We don't have the stomach or conscience to watch it happen. So when people don't have the resources they need to live in retirement, the cost ultimately comes back to all of us as a society to support them. An example of this is the programs in place to support indigent retirees as it relates to prescription drugs. In Pennsylvania, the lottery proceeds are used to pay for prescription drugs for senior citizens who can't afford them. Why not have the employers more fully support in the first place to avoid this issue?

My best example to tangibly demonstrate this concept is the restaurant industry. Restaurant employees are generally not compensated enough to save for retirement, cover major expenses, offered healthcare, etc. As restaurant goers, we help make up for this through tips, but the effects ripple wider. The reality is, not everyone goes to restaurants. While many people do, not everyone does. And when a restaurant worker doesn't have the resources to retire, we as a whole society have to pick up the slack, whether we go to the restaurants or not.

Now, restaurant owners will argue that they'll have to charge $17 instead of $10 (again, making up numbers here) for a pizza in order to support the retirement savings of their employees. This would lead to a drop in sales and potential job cuts.

My argument is that if people aren't willing to pay that $17 for the pizza, then we shouldn't be making the pizza. We should be deploying our resources more efficiently back into society. We don't have enough technicians, plumbers, IT programmers, etc. In that case, we should be redirecting labor to career paths where people are demanding and willing to pay for the services. When we don't deploy our resources the way we should be, we're bastardizing capitalism.

Let me be clear that I'm definitely not advocating that businesses should be forced or regulated into being responsible for helping their employees have sufficient retirement savings. What I am advocating is for business leaders and owners to take their own personal responsibility to not saddle society with problems. While I recognize that I could squeeze a bit more out for myself if I didn't take this approach, at HB Global we choose to align our behavior with our belief system.

Another Perspective – Tammy Halteman

Let's hear from Tammy Halteman, a Human Resources Director at HB Home Services who has been with HB Global for 12 years, for a different perspective on ESOP participation.

1. What does employee ownership mean to you?

> Employee ownership means having both a voice and a responsibility for shaping the future of our company. It's about more than financial ownership, it's about feeling trusted to make decisions, being given the autonomy to lead, and knowing that my contributions directly influence the success we all share. It creates a mindset for me where every choice matters because it impacts not just me, but all of us as owners.

2. What impact has being part of an ESOP had on your life?

> Being part of an ESOP has given me the chance to grow my career in ways I never imagined. I've been trusted with the autonomy to carry out a vision, and that trust has made me more confident, motivated, and invested in the success of the company. On a personal level, knowing that the work I do every day helps build long-term financial security for myself and my fellow employee-owners has been incredibly meaningful.

3. How would you describe the culture of working at an ESOP?

> The culture is collaborative, empowering, and rooted in trust. At an ESOP, people understand that their contributions matter, and that creates a different level of commitment and engagement. Decisions are made with ownership in mind, and there's a strong

sense of shared success. For me, it feels like being part of a workplace where collaboration isn't forced, because we all recognize the direct connection between our individual efforts and our collective success.

Chapter 3
How ESOPs Can Fail

In the early days of ESOPs being a formalized, government-incentivized business structure, there were some highly publicized ESOP failures that made people take a step back and exercise caution. I want to briefly take some time to discuss this before you even have the chance to make this objection and to demonstrate that business failures do not happen solely because a company is formed as an ESOP. There are more fundamental issues at hand.

Yes, ESOPs can fail, but the full context behind why they fail is important. Many times, the reason that an ESOP fails is the same reason that any other business would fail. The same pitfalls that affect non-ESOP public companies and private companies are the same pitfalls that an

ESOP can experience. An ESOP is not a magic elixir. If you decide to take the ESOP route, it doesn't preclude you from making sound business decisions and running your business the same way any other successful business would run. An ESOP adds a layer of complexity, but it doesn't change the fundamentals of running a company.

All that being said, a common way that ESOPs can fail is because they are sold for too high of a purchase price when the ESOP is initially setup. This could be for a couple of reasons. One reason is that the seller is in the middle of a really good economic environment or time period for their business, and they don't consider that things will revert to normal in the future. It's not sustainable for the business to bear the increased debt that results from that. Another reason that ESOPs are sold for too high of a price is because a seller exaggerates the value of the business for their own benefit, saddling the business with exorbitant debt and liabilities that are required to pay that owner.

The first case can be avoided by making sound business decisions as it relates to forecasting and valuation. Even outside of an ESOP, extrapolating a rosy picture when forecasting the future can be problematic. The second case of exaggerating the value of a business would be problematic in any business.

While it's important to ensure that purchase prices for ESOPs are aligned with the market, sellers can structure the deal in a way in which they win over the long term instead of trying a cash grab at the time of sale. By using an earnout, the value they receive for this portion of the purchase price is tied to the future performance of the business. Deals can be structured to include an earnout, and when this is included, the former owner can benefit financially based on the future success of the business. If you are selling to an ESOP, you're confident in the longevity and sustainability of your business, so this earnout makes sense.

When it comes down to it, businesses fail when they aren't generating enough free cash flow to sustain themselves. This can be true of any business that isn't economically sustainable as it's currently formed. Wages could be too high. There could be an underutilization of capacity. A company may require reinvestment that is greater than its cash flow. The list could go on and on.

In *Ownership: Reinventing Companies, Capitalism, and Who Owns What,* Corey Rosen and John Case point to several examples that highlight that businesses generally fail for reasons other than purely being an ESOP. For example, two highly publicized early ESOPs – Rath Packing Company and the National Steel Corporation (later called Weirton) – were already struggling when sold to an ESOP in an effort to turn things around. In the case of Rath Packing, previous ownership hadn't been making the necessary investments to set the company up for success. Weirton experienced difficulties as the steel industry as a whole declined in the US. While they were able to hold on for some time, they eventually sold and restructured in various ways before going bankrupt in 2003.[13] Both of these examples showcase that there are typically other factors coming into play when an ESOP fails, and also that an ESOP isn't a magic, cure-all elixir to fix a company without sound management and cultural components.

Let's look at a few more in-depth examples.

JCPenney – The Fall of a Public Company

JCPenney (JCP) is a clear example of how a public company can fail for the same reasons that an ESOP can. JCP filed for bankruptcy in May of 2020. While it was convenient to blame the pandemic on the need to file for bankruptcy, and while it did serve as the final breaking point, the troubles started long before the pandemic.[14]

The fall of JCP started all the way back during the Great Recession. During that time, they lost many customers to stores with cheaper options. As the economy began to recover, shoppers didn't return. JCP scrambled to try to recover. They brought in new leadership that completely rebranded JCP – the problem was that none of this strategy was market tested. The fall of JCP continued. The old leadership was brought back in to try to stabilize the business. While there was some stabilization, the woes continued. As the old leadership stepped away,

[13] Rosen and Case, *Ownership*: 104–106.

[14] Chris Isidore and Nathaniel Meyersohn, "JCPenney files for bankruptcy," CNN Business, cnn.com, updated May 15, 2020, https://www.cnn.com/2020/05/15/business/jcpenney-bankruptcy/index.html.

another CEO stepped in.[15] In total, JCP had 4 CEOs (in a 10-year timespan!) as it struggled to regain traction before bankruptcy.

Overall, JCP lacked a strategy that had clarity and focus that would allow it to keep up with online retail and big box stores as the brick-and-mortar retail segment faced challenges.[16] JCP tried on several new identities, including appliances and trendier clothing for a younger crowd before realizing they'd strayed too much from their core market.[17]

In many ways, JCP demonstrates how a public company that operates in a struggling industry and doesn't follow sound business practices or establish a clear and effective strategy can fail due to a lack of free cash flow, in the same way that an ESOP can fail as well.

An ESOP Is Not a Magic Fix

A recent ESOP failure that you may be familiar with is that of the Chicago Tribune. In 2007, the Chicago Tribune was converted from a publicly traded company to an ESOP in an $8.2 billion leveraged buyout.[18] As the deal was being put together and executed, the stock price of the Chicago Tribune was falling as newspaper industry stock prices dipped and credit markets began to dry up.[19] By December 2008, the company was filing for bankruptcy protection.[20] Coming out of bankruptcy, the ESOP plan was eliminated.[21] When Chicago Tribune

[15] Nathaniel Meyersohn, "How it all went wrong at JCPenney," CNN Business, cnn.com, updated September 27, 2018, https://www.cnn.com/2018/09/27/business/jcpenney-history/index.html.

[16] Isidore and Meyersohn, "JCPenney files for bankruptcy."

[17] Meyersohn, "How it all went wrong at JCPenney."

[18] Lynne Marek, "Tribune workers get favorable ruling on ESOP suit; company agrees to cut 5 execs from $43M bonus plan," Crain's Chicago Business, chicagobusiness.com, November 10, 2010, https://www.chicagobusiness.com/article/20101110/NEWS06/101119991/tribune-workers-get-favorable-ruling-on-esop-suit-company-agrees-to-cut-5-execs-from-43m-bonus-plan.

[19] Ricard Pérez-Peña, "How Solid Is the Deal for Tribune Company?" *The New York Times*, nytimes.com, August 20, 2007, https://www.nytimes.com/2007/08/20/business/media/20tribune.html.

[20] Marek, "Tribune workers get favorable ruling on ESOP suit."

[21] Michael Oneal, "Tribune to end employee stock ownership plan," *Los Angeles Times*, latimes.com, November 4, 2009, https://www.latimes.com/archives/la-xpm-2009-nov-04-fi-tribune4-story.html.

employees later sued over failed ESOP, the judge ruled that GreatBanc had participated in a prohibited transaction and violated their fiduciary obligations.[22]

This case demonstrates two important points. First, while the ESOP itself failed, there were other contributing factors that led to this failure. The most obvious outside factor was that the country was beginning to fall into the Great Recession in 2007. The second factor was the decline of newspaper industry stocks during the time. This created difficulties for the company that were unrelated to the actual ESOP itself.

The second point is that an ESOP may fail when the deal is not structured appropriately. In the case of the Chicago Tribune, it was highly leveraged, and it was later ruled that GreatBanc violated their fiduciary duties when they approved the leveraged buyout by the ESOP, which turned out to be a prohibited transaction.[23]

Neither of these factors that led to the downfall of the Chicago Tribune as an ESOP company are due to the company becoming an ESOP. Rather, the demise was related to the economic environment and the deal structure. These factors can be problematic for any type of business, not just an ESOP.

On My Soapbox – Capitalism Prevails

A capitalist system is set up so that businesses and industries that are no longer in demand fail. If capital and labor are not being deployed in a way that is productive to society, we redirect the capital and labor to areas where it's better used.

If we, as an ESOP, aren't producing enough free cash flow and value to pay for the retirement needs of our employees, we're pushing the responsibility off to society. Because those employees don't have enough resources, the burden of our errors falls on the healthcare system, the housing system, etc.

[22] Marek, "Tribune workers get favorable ruling on ESOP suit."

[23] Marek, "Tribune workers get favorable ruling on ESOP suit."

Should a company that doesn't produce enough to sustain itself stay in business? I don't think so. A business needs to be able to sustain itself, otherwise, other externalities are created that society pays the price for.

There's an old adage that winners have a tendency to win. I believe that winners win because they are highly attuned to feedback. They notice when something isn't going the way they want it to go, and they adjust. They're attuned to both positive and negative feedback that is received in pursuit of accomplishing their goal.

At HB Global, we've acted on the feedback we've received from acquisitions. Some have been more successful than others, and we've learned from each of those experiences and have seen great success thus far in our most recent acquisitions.

Part of running a business is embodying a winner's mentality and learning from the feedback you receive to improve your decision-making and business practices. And, if you believe you're able to do that successfully over time, you can even benefit after the sale of your ESOP from an earnout portion of the deal.

Becoming an ESOP is not a free pass to a successful business. Sound business practices and fundamentals still need to be applied. The same reasons that a public company can fail are often the same reasons that an ESOP can fail. Whether an ESOP or not, if a company can't produce enough to sustain itself, that capital should be redirected elsewhere for the good of society. Capitalism will prevail.

Another Perspective – David Bellis

Let's hear from David Bellis, Vice President of Construction & Special Projects who has been with HB Global for 29 years, for a different perspective on ESOP participation.

1. What does employee ownership mean to you?

Employee ownership to me means having a stake in the game. I feel employee ownership raises the bar with expectations thus driving results. We strive for excellence, and you can see the results in our teammates, our customers, and in our share price value. The rewards are numerous, and you can feel and see the results every day.

2. What impact has being part of an ESOP had on your life?

The ESOP gives you a stronger retirement foundation and a better sense of financial security.

3. How would you describe the culture of working at an ESOP?

A deeper sense of belonging to a team and being part of something bigger.

Chapter 4
Your Exit Intentions

Having clear intentions as you plan your exit from your business helps mitigate the risk of failure. As we saw in the last chapter, if your intention is to get the highest purchase price and exit as soon as possible, an ESOP may not be right for you. Setting exit intentions positions you, your business, and your employees for success. While many people think of this as they near the end of their careers, it's never too early to start examining and planning for your succession. Let's take a look at the story of Cliff Nash.

Nash Plumbing & Mechanical (PM) was a family-owned business in Central Florida. When we acquired this business, it was run by Cliff Nash. The business had grown significantly since the time he had bought his dad out in the 1990s and, by the mid-2010s, was a $30 – $40 million revenue business – pushing $50 million some years.

Even with this size and scope of the business, Cliff was still personally signing for payment and performance bonds (i.e. basically a type of insurance used in the construction industry) and putting his personal assets on the line. There were times when things were tough, and he had to re-mortgage his house. But he made sure employees at his company never missed a paycheck. He was proud of this but took on a lot of stress by taking personal responsibility for this size commercial construction business.

In 2014, the stress caught up to Cliff. He went into atrial fibrillation (AFib). It took three days to get his heart back into rhythm. Prior to this incident, Cliff had never spent a day of his life in the hospital. The doctor made it clear to Cliff that his stress levels were the cause of the AFib. He was straightforward in saying that Cliff either needed to back down from his current stress level and capacity at his business or the stress would kill him.

With the size of the business, it would've taken a pretty healthy loan or line of credit for Cliff to be bought out. The senior leadership team at the time was at the end of their careers and wouldn't be up for taking on a long-term note. This left things up to Cliff's son, Ryan. However, neither Cliff nor Ryan wanted to take on the stress of Ryan stepping into the ownership role. Ryan wanted to avoid the high stress he saw his dad go through. Cliff didn't want his son to go through that and also knew he wouldn't be able to fully disconnect if his son bought him out.

Cliff and Ryan agreed that the best path forward was to find an agent and quietly put the business on the market. While they were listing the business, their intention was to find an opportunity where Ryan Nash could still run it.

They had a few investors who were interested, but most of the initial interest came from private equity (PE) roll-ups who wanted Nash PM to grow in Central Florida but not expand beyond that. This left a bad taste with Cliff and Ryan because they knew they would've been out of business various times by then if they'd followed that philosophy.

When we noticed the Nash PM listing, we saw a lot of growth opportunities. It was an opportunity for us to expand into Florida, but it was also an opportunity for Nash PM to expand their geography as well as step into special projects and service offerings. Cliff and Ryan felt joining our family of brands would be a good cultural fit and allow them to accomplish the goals they had for both themselves and the employees upon exit. Ryan would get a chance to run the business, Cliff would be on the Board of Directors, and the employees would be taken care of through the ESOP structure in a culture that was aligned with their existing business.

In 2017, we completed the acquisition of Nash PM. It's worth noting that, although his employees would've been taken care of through the structure of the acquisition, Cliff took a substantial amount of his purchase price and paid bonuses to his employees as well to thank them for their dedication. This is a clear demonstration of the character of Cliff, his desire to make sure his employees were taken care of, and why an ESOP was such a great cultural fit for his exit.

The acquisition was wildly successful. Ryan is now our division president at Nash PM, Cliff is still on our board, and the employees have benefited even beyond what they received in share value. Nash PM has been able to take on more risk since it wouldn't all fall back on Cliff's personal assets, which allowed them to expand geographically and take on bolder projects. The acquisition set them up to be the best versions of themselves.

****

A key aspect of understanding if an ESOP is right for you is to understand your exit intentions. Frequently, business owners don't consider their exit intentions or succession planning in a sufficient amount of time. It's never too early to start being intentional about your transition plan, especially because you never know when the unexpected may happen.

While things worked out for Nash PM, there are a few points of this story that demonstrate the importance of establishing exit intentions early. The most obvious is perhaps the reminder that the unexpected can happen at any time. Cliff had been a completely healthy man before the stress caught up to him. Not a day in the hospital beforehand is a pretty impressive record. All parties are able to better navigate the unexpected if thoughtful and intentional planning has been done beforehand.

The second important takeaway from this story is the amount of time and planning that an exit transition takes. Cliff's hospitalization took place in 2014. It wasn't until November of 2017 that we ended up acquiring Nash PM. The time for Cliff to exit the business still ended up being a few years even after a visit to the emergency room and the fateful proclamation from his doctor. And the transition didn't stop after the acquisition. We were fortunate that Cliff and Ryan had clear intentions when they did decide to exit and had the benefit of Ryan wanting to stay on and eventually run the subsidiary as well as Cliff continuing to be a guiding Board member.

Why Setting Intentions Early is Important

Setting exit intentions prior to reaching retirement age is critical. We've already demonstrated this through Cliff's story and the potential of the unexpected to pop up. But even if everything is carrying on as expected, setting intentions early is the key to a successful transition.

To transition a lower/middle market business, there is generally a long lead time to do it successfully. For these types of businesses, it's ideal to have at least 10 years of planning. It can be done successfully in five years if necessary, but even then, you aren't jumping right into a transition once you make the decision to exit. These time frames aren't universal truths but generally hold true for a smooth and successful transition and a sustainable business after exit. So why does it take so long?

There are several considerations to make when exiting and transitioning a business. It's important to start by being thoughtful about what you want to accomplish during your time with the business and what you want the business to accomplish after your exit. Identifying personal goals and business goals for the long term is a great place to start. This takes time though. Thoughtful goals require significant contemplation and, in a business setting, collaboration with others.

Once your goals have been identified, it takes time to get things in place to accomplish those goals. This starts by positioning the business for value and sustainability. How much value? Depends on your goals. But giving yourself sufficient runway is what will allow you the time to accumulate the necessary financial resources.

Another key to a successful transition is having a successor leader in place. This is a key aspect of what made the Nash PM acquisition so successful. Cliff and Ryan had set the intention that Ryan still desired to run the business. Ryan was a few years away from being ready to run the business. Cliff's second-in-command, Dave Mears III, was ready and willing to run the business and work to prepare Ryan to lead. Within three years of our acquisition, Ryan took the helm. He used his years of cultural and technical knowledge of the business to make the transition as seamless as possible.

It generally takes time to get this successor leader in place. The first step is identifying a successor leader. This typically doesn't happen overnight. Once this individual is identified, it takes time to immerse them in the go-forward vision for the company in facets such as the mission of the company, the culture, key partnerships, etc. It also takes time to ensure that the leader of the business will carry it forward in a way that is aligned with your intentions as an exiting owner.

All these preparatory steps are usually benefited by having a diverse group of people involved who are responsible for making the planning and transition happen. This doesn't just result in more points of view being brought to the table, but it actually increases the value of the business. It makes the business more sustainable by removing the dependency on one person, and the business is also perceived as being more valuable when there are several key, knowledgeable players.

There's one more reason setting early exit intentions is important, and it's completely intangible. That reason is mental preparation. Completing the transition of a business is generally traumatic. As a business owner, you've invested immense time and energy in building up the business. You probably start to identify with it as a reflection of you. And outside of yourself, your family is likely invested in it as well. They've lived these formative years of the business with you and have enjoyed the success of the business; the transition impacts them both financially and emotionally. Taking time to prepare, especially with a group, allows the exiting owner, the family of the owner, and the employees to more easily navigate this transition. Without proper planning, trust can be broken.

Building Trust

Depending on the exit intention that is chosen, early planning and a thoughtful transition help to build trust, which is crucial to the sustainability and success of the business. I believe, aside from a dire turnaround situation where urgent action is needed, it's a universal truth that when somebody comes into a new situation, the very first thing that they need to do is build trust with the constituency of people that they're going to be working with. Having a thoughtfully planned transition or exit plan helps this to happen because of the time it takes.

I am confident the best thing I did when I came into HB McClure was that I took my time, listened, and didn't do much in the early stages other than try to understand the business. When I did pick things to tackle after some time, they were really low-hanging fruit, because I had taken the time to build trust.

In my case, I believe that this was actually by accident. I was way too young and thought way too highly of myself that I would have done that on purpose. I did it because I came into a totally new industry that I didn't know squat about, and I was at least self-aware enough to realize that. I was humble enough to realize this business was different from the industries I was accustomed to, and I figured I had better listen and learn before I started making changes.

But if I had gone into the employee benefits brokerage industry that I had been in before, I can almost guarantee that I would have gone into the business saying, "This is the right way to do this, and we need to implement that here," or "This is how I've done things in the past." If that had been the case, I would have been spit out right away just like so many of the other leaders I see that come in like a wrecking ball trying to make immediate changes before building trust.

The best way to build trust in a new situation is to open up your ears and listen, for the primary purpose of building trust. When a transition is thoughtfully and intentionally planned, new ownership or leadership gains the opportunity to do this without being thrown into a fire drill situation. When trust isn't built first, new ideas are met with resistance. They could be great ideas, but the apprehension is there from the constituents of the business because there's no trust built up yet. Richard Ruback and Royce Yudkoff echo this sentiment in their book *HBR Guide to Buying a Small Business* and their podcast *Think Big, Buy Small,* promoting the idea that when owners buy a business, they shouldn't be in a rush to change things. They even mention that most of their Harvard grads dive into making change before building this trust. (The Big Red has gotta get a dig in on the Crimson when we can because we don't get very many opportunities!)

How and when trust is established is a case-by-case basis, which is why it's also important to identify your current state and intentions in transition. We have a great example of that with one of the leaders in our company. We put this leader in charge of one of our subsidiaries that had basically never made money. This leader came in and took his time to listen and evaluate the situation. This was paired with the fact that the other leaders knew they needed some help. So this leader, after assessing the situation, was able to make some changes to help this company now thrive.

After this success, we transferred this same leader to run a different subsidiary. Because of his success at the prior subsidiary, he came in overconfident and started trying to make changes immediately. Not only had his approach shifted from first listening, but this was also accompanied by the fact that this particular subsidiary was more seasoned and had been around the block. The desire to make all these changes right off the bat was met with much resistance. This leader has since realized their shortcomings and has taken a step back, recognizing the importance of building trust.

I've seen this situation play out time and time again. Many leaders learn through experience the importance of building trust. If they don't come in with that as a priority, the good ones will realize the importance of it, take a step back, and focus on establishing that trust.

The bad ones will continue to push forward without trust and will be chewed up and spit out.

As a leader of your business, you can help others be set up for success by creating a situation in which they are able to take their time to build trust, which ultimately benefits the employees and all shareholders involved.

On My Soapbox – Independence from the Owner

As an owner of a business, the business needs to have as little dependence on you as possible. This is counterintuitive for most business owners, but for the business to be successful over multiple generations, it's necessary for sustainability.

The ability of a business to be able to operate independently from its owner takes time, though. In most cases, the owner was and is the driving force behind building the business. So logistically, it takes time to develop a strategy in which the business gains independence from the owner and for the appropriate individuals to take on leadership roles.

But this also takes mental preparation and awareness from the business owner's perspective. In many cases, the business is tied to the owner's ego. The owner of the business views the success of the business as a reflection on them. So the struggle becomes: what happens to us as business owners when the business isn't dependent on us anymore?

I'll admit that I struggle with this as well. My ego is tied to the success of this business. I get upset when things don't go the way I envision them going because I ultimately feel it's a reflection on me. Now, everyone has different scorecards for success. In my case, success for our business means fulfilling our mission to make HB Global a great place to work and create value for our employee owners.

I'll use an analogy that shows the dichotomy between being a business owner and being a parent. As parents, we try to remove ourselves from feeling that our children are a reflection on us. Our intent is to raise children who decide for themselves what impact they want to make on the world. While we may guide them to help set them up for success, we ultimately want them to be independent and make the decisions that fulfill them. I don't want mini-me's for kids, but I do for my business.

A business is a different animal because it's inanimate. I want the business to survive me, but I want the business to survive with the same mission that it was built on during my time as CEO. The greatness of our business is judged upon its ability to execute our mission over multiple generations. Jim Collins talks about this in his books. While we try to avoid this as parents, most people do view the success of their business as a reflection on them.

This can be positive or negative. To the extent that business owners and leaders use it for the greater good, it's a positive thing. However, to the extent that it is used to make egos feel good, it's a negative thing.

Nevertheless, almost universally, a business needs to be able to operate independently from its owner for the owner to successfully exit down the road. This takes time to put the strategy in place. It takes time to do succession planning to groom leaders who will carry on the mission of the business. And it takes time for the owner to adapt to this mindset as well. This is why early planning is so essential to a successful transition.

Another Perspective – Cliff Nash and Ryan Nash

We sought Cliff Nash's reaction and feedback to sharing his story in this book, and he provided a valuable reflection on his journey.

"As I began to read the opening of the Nash PM chapter, it brought back memories both good and bad of the very difficult time of transition in my life that not only affected my family (Susan, Ryan, and my brother George) but also my second family at Nash PM. This is what made it so difficult to make a decision regarding the best plan to exit the business and set Susan and I up for the next chapter in our lives while also allowing the Nash PM family to continue to flourish and not miss a beat, as if nothing had changed.

It was important to me for my son, Ryan, and all our key employees to be on board with this sale. The buyer had to be on board with the same values and goals that we had currently as a family-owned business that cared deeply for its employees and what was in store for them in the future after the sale was complete.

Well, this is what we got with Bob Whalen and the HB McClure group. I could not have asked for a better answer to my prayers. Although we had our moments during the negotiations and preparation for the sale, the process went well. I found during this process how, in fact, our values aligned, and this made for an easy transition into the new family.

Looking back, I have no regrets about our company becoming part of the HB Global group of companies. I am so proud of Ryan and the entire Nash PM family for what they have done to make the company a jewel in the crown of HB Global. I would have never in my wildest dreams have thought that this would have been so successful... WOW.

It was Bob's dream to create a workplace where all employees have an opportunity to be owners and benefit from their hard work, and it seems to be working well at HB Global!!

I am proud to still be part of the team as a board member and enjoy watching the continued success and transitions going on to make this a great company."

His son, Ryan, who is now President of Nash PM, had this to say:

"I am very thankful for the support the entire team has given me to be able to continue to run the business with such autonomy. Bob and the capital behind the HB shield have enabled us to grow our business to a position that I never would have thought of. It has been an incredible journey that I am very proud of for our business and our employees here."

Chapter 5
Alternative Options

When it comes to big decisions like exiting your business, there isn't one objectively right answer. That's why setting intentions prior to an exit is so key. While I'm a huge advocate for ESOPs, there are many ways to exit a business depending on what your priorities are for your exit. Some options are widely known, but some may surprise you.

In 2022, we started HB Capital. HB Capital buys companies in a similar way to any other private equity (PE) fund, with one major difference: we are committed to an ESOP exit. While it would've been great for HB Global to continue to acquire businesses to allow them to become ESOPs, HB Global reached a maturity level where it didn't make sense for the company to take on the level of financial risk that it had earlier in its life cycle. While HB Global still acquires companies that are in alignment with its risk tolerance and strategy, HB Capital is positioned to take on the financial risk of buying companies to eventually help them exit to an ESOP.

HB Capital has an expertise that investors are willing to pay for. The best part is that employees at HB Global reap the benefits of HB Capital as well. HB Global is also an investor in HB Capital because it is committed to creating value for employee owners and is aligned with the goals and missions of HB Capital.

So while HB Capital helps to diversify and expand opportunities at HB Global, it also helps solve an important problem for exiting owners. HB Capital helps business owners exit to an ESOP without needing the five to ten years of exit planning. HB Capital takes on the financial burden and risk of what is entailed with becoming an ESOP and also helps owners not need to make a split decision to sell to a buyer that may not be a good fit but is right in front of them.

HB Capital provides exiting owners with many of the benefits and conveniences of exiting to a PE firm while still knowing that their employees will be taken care of, rather than just being part of another future transaction. We have a unique sourcing advantage because of our commitment to exit to an ESOP. True to our values at HB Global, HB Capital is transparent with exiting owners and investors that we won't just sell to the highest bidder but instead will sell to a reputable ESOP. This transparency up front sets appropriate expectations and our commitment to this helps us to maintain trust and our sourcing advantage. The investors in HB Capital know what they're getting – exits to ESOPs but not necessarily top dollar.

PE firms often get a bad reputation. But in reality, they are often working quickly and selling to the highest bidder because of a fiduciary duty to their investors. Some PE firms are now trying to take care of employees by distributing bonuses to all employees based on the success of the PE firm sale. We've adopted that at HB Capital, too.

HB Capital is unique in its mission and its execution. While it's a great option for some business owners, it's not right for everyone. The world is ripe with different options for how you may want to exit your business. If financial return is your highest priority, you probably want to exit to a traditional PE firm or a strategic buyer who will pay for "synergies." If keeping a business in the family is a priority, exiting to the next generation makes sense. If you want to exit your current business structure but still have control of taking care of your employees, ESOPs are a great option. Different options will lead you to different outcomes, and there isn't a one-size-fits-all answer. Your goals should drive your decisions.

I'm a big proponent of ESOPs, but I don't believe this option is necessarily the "right" option for everyone nor do I intend to force it on anyone. So in this chapter, we'll spend some time exploring alternative exit options. It's important to note that this is not an exhaustive list, and additional research should be done on the pros and cons of each option or other options available.

Private Equity

We've compared HB Capital to PE firms, so let's talk at a very high level about what it means to sell to a PE firm. When an owner sells to a PE firm, they are selling to an institutional owner that the business then has to answer to. In most cases, a significant amount of autonomy is lost.

Almost all PE options are time-limited, meaning the PE firm will again look to transact the business in three to five, potentially up to ten years from now (although ten years is a long time in the PE world). Because of the time-bound nature of most deals, the PE firm will be looking to make changes in short order to increase the value of the business for sale within that time frame. The PE firm can then sell to a variety of buyers, including options like another PE firm, a strategic buyer, or an individual.

However, there is a new strategy that is gaining momentum in the private equity world to help better take care of employees. In this new strategy, PE firms are sharing the success of the exit transaction with all employees. This means that the PE firm is paying employees a percentage of the proceeds when the business is again sold. This helps the employees to share in the value created while the PE firm owned the company, which makes the company quasi-employee-owned for the period of time when working with PE firms that deploy this strategy. This strategy was popularized by Ownership Works, a not-for-profit organization, but is picking up steam with some other PE firms.

A PE firm is often the alternative of choice for owners who are looking to quickly exit the business and who have the priority of getting the highest financial return from selling. However, the world of PE firms is vast, and the pros and cons of selling to a PE firm will vary depending on the goals of each firm and owner.

Sell to an Individual Who Wants to Buy and Operate a Business

I ended up at HB McClure because I wanted to buy and operate a business. It wasn't because I was intent on turning the company into an ESOP. We know that came later because it was a practical solution that highly aligned with my personal goals for the company. But when I first started my journey, HB McClure was a highly respected company in the town I was from that was for sale, and I felt honored to have the opportunity to carry on the legacy of the blue and yellow trucks that had always been known in the area.

Selling to an individual who wants to buy and operate a business is one option for transitioning your company. These individuals typically fall into two different categories. The first category is someone like me who wants the chance to operate a business and is looking for options that they may know and love. Then there's a universe of Searchers.

Searchers are typically graduates from MBA programs looking to find a business to run. These Searchers can be funded in a variety of different ways. They typically have investors who are delivering the equity capital needed to do the deal and are putting some amount of leverage on the company. Some Searchers will look to increase the value of the business and exit with their investors within a few years, like a PE firm. Other Searchers will play the long game, operate the business long-term, and find a way to get their investors out in the future.

Even within this one exit alternative, the potential options for how this may play out are extensive. The outcomes of this option are really dependent on the goals of the individual looking to buy.

Strategic Buyers

Aside from individuals, there are also what's commonly referred to as strategic buyers. These are typically companies within your industry that are often competitors of yours. They may or may not be in your market. Often, they want to combine businesses to expand in some way and create some synergies within the business.

For example, in 2020, T-Mobile acquired Sprint. At the time, T-Mobile was the third-largest wireless carrier, and Sprint was the fourth-largest wireless carrier. The two companies entered into this deal to become more formidable competition against the top two wireless carriers.[24]

Every industry has these strategic buyers, and they could come in a variety of forms. They may be publicly traded or they may be privately owned. These strategic buyers could also be conglomerates – although that is less common these days. When a conglomerate is a strategic buyer, they are often looking for a business outside of what they do today.

We even have an example of this going back several decades in the HB McClure history. In 1952, the McClure family had started the McClure Company, focused on commercial mechanical and electrical contracting. This created two facets of HB McClure: the McClure Company and HB McClure. In 1984, the family decided to make a clear separation between the two companies with Bill McClure, Jr. taking ownership of the McClure Company, and Bob McClure taking ownership of HB McClure. In 1998, Bill Jr. sold his majority ownership position in the McClure Company to Pennsylvania Power & Light (PP&L). PP&L was a strategic buyer looking to create a complete client solution through creating synergies and offerings in both HVAC infrastructure and electrical solutions. Many in the industry across the nation found this acquisition to be innovative.

[24] Daniel Liberto, "Strategic Buyer: Meaning, Criticism, and Example," investopedia.com, July 10, 2023, https://www.investopedia.com/terms/s/strategic-buyer.asp#citation-5.

These types of acquisitions are still prevalent today across industries. In 2021, Salesforce acquired Slack Technologies, Inc. as a strategic move that would allow the CRM company to obtain a digital platform that allowed employees to stay connected in a remote work world. This strategy was deployed to help "give every company in the world a single source of truth for their business and a single platform for connecting employees, customers, and partners with each other and the apps they use every day."[25]

Similar to individuals, different strategic buyers will have different goals. In order to understand the potential costs and benefits, it's important to understand the intentions of the strategic buyer.

Transition to Family

If you're an owner who wants to protect the longevity and legacy of the business you've built, a desirable outcome may be to sell to your family. This is a way to pass the company down to future generations that you trust to run the business in a way that is aligned with how you'd run the business.

In this case, the family members of choice would buy out the existing ownership. This is a great option if future generations of the family are interested in being involved in keeping the business going.

SC Johnson is an example of a family-owned business that you may not expect. They are a privately held company with a centralized ownership model. SC Johnson was established in 1886 and has maintained family leadership through five generations, with a family leader that has voting control and a family council as well as a board of directors.[26]

[25] "Salesforce Completes Acquisition of Slack," salesforce.com, July 21, 2021, https://www.salesforce.com/news/press-releases/2021/07/21/salesforce-slack-deal-close/.

[26] Rob Sligh, "Succession: The Transfer of Power in Family Businesses," The Family Business Consulting Group, thefbcg.com, January 7, 2025, https://www.thefbcg.com/resource/succession-the-transfer-of-power-in-family-businesses/#:~:text=SC%20Johnson%20is%20an%20example,companies%20in%20the%20United%20States.

Management Buyout

Future generations or other family members may not have the desire, however, to work within or run the family business. However, the exiting owner may still have a desire for a trusted individual or individuals to run the business to protect the legacy of the company.

In that case, the exiting owner may consider a management buyout. This is similar to transitioning to family members, but in this case, members of the management team are buying out the exiting owner.

Shutdown and Liquidation

As an option of last resort, exiting owners may consider shutting down the business and liquidating the assets. There are a whole host of circumstances that may give rise to this option. In this alternative, the exiting owner doesn't benefit from the purchase price of some individual or entity buying the business. Instead, they try to get any liquidity they can from selling off the assets.

Many situations in which this occurs are a case-by-case basis, but an example we can talk about here is a business operating in a suffering industry. When a business is operating in a declining industry, it's unlikely that there are going to be buyers lined up at the door willing to pay a fair price. In this case, the exiting owner may get more value from selling off the property or the building to a completely different business. For example, a building or land in a high-traffic area could have more value than the business itself.

Sell Your Business to an ESOP Trust

Even within the world of ESOPs, there are a variety of options. While there are unique circumstances like HB Capital, there are two main ways to transition your business to an ESOP. The first one we'll discuss is selling your business to an ESOP trust, which is the path that I took with HB McClure.

The primary advantage of selling to an ESOP trust is that you maintain almost the same level of control that you had when you owned the business outright. If you as an owner are looking to retire rather than run the business yourself, you still have control over succession planning and who continues to run the business.

When a business is sold to an ESOP trust, the business will have a Board of Directors that has the same responsibilities as any other company. One additional layer of oversight that is added when selling to an ESOP trust is that there will also be a trustee who represents the ESOP shareholders. This trustee needs to approve certain decisions, such as certain asset divestitures, but for the most part, the Board and the CEO maintain much of the control of the business they are operating. In many of the other alternatives we've discussed, this level of control would be given up.

Businesses of all shapes and sizes can take this approach. Even Publix, with over 260,000 employees, participates in an ESOP.[27] They are the largest majority employee-owned company in the country.[28]

For the technicalities regarding the process and details related to selling to an ESOP trust, reference the appendix for more information and resources.

Sell to an ESOP Company

Another way for your company to transition to an ESOP is to sell to an already existing ESOP company. This ESOP company could be a strategic buyer explained earlier or it could be a holding company. HB Global is an example of a holding company that houses a variety of subsidiaries based on the companies we acquire. Because we are an ESOP, the employees within the acquired business become part of our ESOP plan. This isn't just true at HB Global but is true any time that a business is sold to an existing ESOP company.

[27] "Facts & Figures," Publix, corporate.publix.com, accessed October 31, 2025, https://corporate.publix.com/about-publix/company-overview/facts-figures.

[28] "The Employee Ownership 100," The National Center for Employee Ownership, nceo.org, updated October 2025, https://www.nceo.org/research/employee-ownership-100-largest-employee-owned-companies.

However, the owner does lose a certain amount of control in this case. This is similar to selling to a strategic buyer. The amount of lost control will be dependent on the purchasing company, but in any case, there will be loss of control to a certain extent. For example, at HB Global, we try to give our acquired subsidiaries as much autonomy as possible. They know their customers, markets, and services best. However, when it gets down to it, we ultimately have the right to make decisions for them or implement certain processes or guidelines. They are still accountable to HB Global as a holding company.

Selling to another ESOP company works best when there is a cultural alignment between the company being sold, the exiting owner, and the ESOP company that is looking to acquire. The culture of an ESOP is particularly important because the value creation and sharing is dependent on the success of the team, so it's important to ensure alignment when considering this option.

On My Soapbox – Loss of Control

An underappreciated consideration when planning the sale of your business is the amount of control you give up in each alternative option. As you've seen throughout the chapter, there are a variety of options that create a spectrum of how much control is retained or lost. We have selling outright to someone like a strategic buyer or individual on one end of the spectrum and then we have selling your business to an ESOP trust on the other end of the spectrum.

An owner's satisfaction after the sale of their business is dependent on whether the amount of control they gave up is aligned with their goals and intentions for their exit. Some people want to shake their hands and be free and clear of the business. For other people, it's their baby, and they want to maintain as much control as possible.

There's no right or wrong answer here. The key takeaway is that you take an honest look at what's most important to you when selling your business. While there are many tactical considerations, potentially the most important consideration is how much control you want to retain because that will end up driving all strategic decisions.

Another Perspective – Russel P. Nash

Let's hear from Russell P. Nash, former owner of William R. Nash, who decided to sell his company to HB Global in 2020.

1. What were your priorities when selling your company?

We had three main priorities when finding a buyer for our company:

1. Achieving maximum value in the selling price.

2. Finding a buyer who was interested in making a long-term commitment (e.g. No private equity need apply) in growing the organization and conducting business that was also focused on the welfare of our employees in its decision making.

3. Finding a buyer who would continue our organization's focus on "Teamwork, Pride & Quality" while still providing a first-class safety program for our people and not tarnishing our reputation or our name.

2. How did it feel selling your company to an ESOP?

In our mind, that checked the box for priority #2 and then some. For our employees to be able to benefit financially as partial owners while the company continued to succeed was a huge reason why we sold to HB.

3. How would you describe the success and legacy of your business today?

In these past 5 years since the sale, the company has flourished and grown as an organization beyond my expectations (and I believe HB's as well) and has continued to be a major player in providing mechanical construction services in the South Florida & U.S. Virgin Islands marketplace. No regrets!

Chapter 6
The Flexibility of an ESOP

From 2010 to 2017, we were 100% ESOP-owned. In 2017, we made the decision to shift our structure to only being 80% ESOP-owned by having the executive team buy additional management shares in the company. At this point in the book, that decision may surprise you, so let's talk about why we did it.

By 2017, our business was growing in sophistication. We had made our second major acquisition, and we were contemplating pursuing the roll-up strategy that we employ today. An increase in sophistication meant our executive class was taking on more responsibility. We wanted our executives to have more of a tie to the stock performance in their compensation, and it was also important to me that they got rewarded for their increase in accountability. To enable our executives to buy the management shares, we gave them a loan to buy the shares, and we bonused them over time to pay that loan back.

My priority is always taking care of our employees, and that means taking care of all employees throughout the organization. Furthermore, the management shares allowed us to institute more sophisticated long-term incentive plans that aligned with the increasing complexity of our organization.

Our story is just one example of the large amount of flexibility that ESOPs allow. While there are many guidelines and regulations that govern ESOPs, there is also immense flexibility. In this chapter, we'll cover some other common areas of flexibility allowed within an ESOP. This only provides a high-level overview. We also recognize that the landscape of regulations is ever-changing. Please consult professional ESOP and tax advisors for the most accurate and representative information for your specific case and questions.

ESOP Plan Design Features

When establishing or converting to an ESOP, a plan document will need to be created that will outline the operation of the ESOP. There are many potential features as it relates to ESOP plan design. The first decision that will need to be made is if you want to create your own plan or if you want to adopt an already established plan. At HB Global, we began by creating a customized plan that was approved by the IRS, but we later adopted a standardized plan pre-approved by the IRS when our plan document was required to be renewed per regulatory guidance. While the list of potential plan design features is long, here are some decisions that need to be made as it relates to ESOP plan design:[29]

- Who will participate in the plan?
- How will the stock be allocated to participants?
- What vesting schedule will apply to any employer contributions to the plan?
- How will distributions of ESOP accounts be handled?

[29] The ESOP Association, "How to Establish an ESOP," esopassociation.org, November 18, 2019, https://www.esopassociation.org/articles/how-to-establish-an-esop.

- How will voting rights be handled?
- Will the ESOP have an internal trustee or a professional independent trustee?

These questions scratch the surface but are great to get you started. When it came to our plan design at HB Global, there were over 20 different decisions that we had to make for how our ESOP plan would operate. This may vary as it relates to the size, complexity, and approach to your ESOP, but it demonstrates the various points of flexibility within a plan. I am sparing you the technical details of those decisions as the goal of this book isn't to help put you to sleep at night. I will, however, give you a brief overview of some of the common ones.

It's Not All or Nothing

Our story of evolution at HB Global demonstrates the first principle of flexibility within an ESOP: it's not all or nothing. It's possible for anywhere from 1% to 100% of the company to be ESOP-owned. There are different benefits, especially as it relates to taxes, to different levels of ESOP ownership. It's best to consult with an expert to discuss what may be best for your situation.

Technically, being structured as an ESOP doesn't create a tax-free situation. Rather, the taxes are deferred in some sense. As discussed earlier, the taxes are paid when ESOP balances are distributed to their participants. The difference is that this is not a perfect correlation for not paying taxes on profits over the decades it is in operation, thereby greatly reducing the overall tax burden. The participants pay ordinary income on these distributions, rather than paying corporate tax rates. The tax-deferred nature of ESOPs allows transitioning owners to use short-term tax savings to pay a portion of the purchase price or the price to convert the business. This tax efficiency also allows for flexibility in the business in the long-term to direct funds to key priorities of the business.

In some cases, when owners are looking to convert their business to an ESOP, they will do this in two transactions. They will first sell typically 30% to 40% of the business to the ESOP to get liquidity from the transaction, which is funded solely with senior debt so that the seller gets all cash at close. This also allows owners to get a better feel for what it's like being an ESOP before completing a full conversion. When an ESOP owns less than 50% of the company, it's going to be discounted when sold because of the minority ownership. So owners need to decide if they want to sell more than 50% right away and not get a minority discount while they're still working to understand the ESOP structure.

NewAge Industries Case Study

One of my favorite examples of a company using a phased, or tranched, ESOP approach is NewAge Industries. Ken Baker, former CEO and now Chairman of the company, was gracious enough to take us through his journey.

NewAge is a plastic tubing manufacturer based in Southampton, PA and was started back in 1954 by Ken's father, Ray Baker. Eventually, Ken and his brother joined their dad in operating the business. Ken was intrigued by the concept of Total Quality Management and was looking for ways to improve the business. As he researched paths he could take, he received a mailer from the National Center for Employee Ownership and decided to attend the conference. After learning about employee ownership, Ken saw that it would be a great way to buy out his father's and brother's stake in the company while also improving the business overall.

Ken pursued this route and admitted that he wasn't crazy about the first valuation and share price. After careful consideration, he moved forward with selling 30% of the company to an ESOP in 2006 to test the waters of employee ownership. This gave him the liquidity he needed to buy out his dad and brother while also allowing him to receive the tax benefits provided by the federal government for ESOPs.

Ken fully embraced the employee ownership culture. He operated with a "Management by Walking Around" (MBWA) style where he'd be sure to greet employees on the shop floor each day. Kevin McPhillips, Executive Director and CEO of the Pennsylvania Center for Employee Ownership (PaCEO), noted that Ken was a tremendous leader who struck a balance of being hands-on where needed but delegating well to let each employee shine. He would remind employees as well about their ownership role. As he walked around the shop floor one day, a forklift operator was laying a patch (meaning the tires were skidding), leaving marks on the floor and dust all over the warehouse, not to mention wearing out the tires. Ken approached the employee, who we'll call Joe, and said, "Joe, why are you beating up your forklift? I have a better question for you. Why are you beating up Sue's forklift?" Joe's head fell as the realization sank in. Ken ensured that all employees looked at their work as owners of the company.

Once Ken got into employee ownership, he continued to see the benefits and felt it was a good idea to keep moving forward with it. He considered a strategy to continue increasing the employee ownership of the company. In 2013, Ken sold a second 10% tranche to the ESOP so that 40% of the company would now be employee-owned. Because the company was doing so well, the 10% was valued at a much higher share price than the original 30%, and this increase in value validated the decision Ken had made to move forward with his original decision towards employee ownership.

Three years later, Ken decided to sell an additional 9% of the company to the ESOP, which meant the ESOP would own 49% of the company. This was a calculated decision to ensure the ESOP trust would still own a minority of the company. As Ken's company grew like crazy and adjusted to the idea of employee ownership, he wanted to maintain control of the Board of Directors who would help guide the direction of the company. Kevin McPhillips provided his expertise on this topic. He explained that once the employees own more than 50% of the company, the trustee can get legal control to appoint the Board of Directors.

In 2019, Ken saw that the business was doing great, a huge enterprise of over 200 employees had been built, and everyone was really happy. After having reflected on this, Ken decided to sell the remaining 51% of the company to the ESOP so that it would be 100% employee owned. He set up a meeting with all the employees and made the announcement. It was a joyous occasion! The employees really appreciated Ken's actions and recognized that they would be financially fruitful in a world where so many don't have sufficient funds for retirement.

The company has seen great success since becoming 100% ESOP-owned. There are two hallmark events that demonstrate this success. The first came in 2020, when the company was put to the test. NewAge has a high-quality medical pharmaceutical division as well as RFD tagging technology. As COVID wreaked havoc in 2020, NewAge was called upon to ramp up production. They had many clients in the pharmaceutical and medical fields. Their products would be used to supply equipment that would help with lung treatments and other crucial treatments. NewAge even received a quota from the federal government to produce a certain amount of tubing in a certain amount of time and delivered when many other businesses were unable to.

The second hallmark event that reflects the success and growth of the company and employees is international expansion and opening up a division in the Netherlands.

One ancillary benefit of taking the phased approach was that each time Ken sold another tranche, it was at a much higher share price than the previous tranche sold for. This meant that he was able to sell the business over time for much more than he would've gotten if he would've sold the business outright. That was part of Ken's strategy of selling the business in tranches because he knew he could grow the business.

Ken's intentions aligned perfectly with the benefits that employee ownership would provide to his company. As the company celebrated 15 years of being an ESOP, Ken explained that he'd had hundreds of offers to sell to other businesses but had this to say, "What's the easiest way to squash your competition or to expand your product offering? Buy another company. But I didn't want to take the money that was being offered and walk away from the business my father started in 1954. NewAge has been part of my life almost as far back as I can remember. My father and I and my family put a lot of hours and sweat equity into growing NewAge. And there are people who've worked here for 20, 25, 30 years. I wanted to reward them in a meaningful way for their hard work, dedication and loyalty." The website notes that the share price had appreciated 975% over those 15 years (2006 – 2021)![30]

[30] "NewAge® Industries Observes 15 Years of Employee Ownership," NewAge Industries, newageindustries.com, January 12, 2021, https://newageindustries.com/newage-industries-observes-15-years-of-employee-ownership/.

Ken and Kevin now promote awareness and provide education around ESOPs and employee ownership as co-founders of the Pennsylvania Center for Employee Ownership. They've also launched the Baker Project (bakerproject.org) to raise awareness and education related to employee ownership.

Executive Compensation

As companies evolve in sophistication, the ESOP structure is able to evolve with them. We demonstrated that with our shift in 2017 as it relates to how much of HB Global was ESOP-owned. This is an incredibly valuable component of the ESOP structure because, as businesses evolve in sophistication, executive talent that can manage that sophistication needs to be brought on board. It's important that ESOPs can be competitive in attracting the appropriate team.

In the United States, the annual compensation limit for 401(k), profit sharing, etc. plans is $350,000 as of 2025.[31] Anyone making over that amount can't earn a proportional amount of ESOP shares for what they earn. This is an important consideration in attracting executive talent. The fact of the matter is that companies need to compete in the marketplace for leadership talent, especially considering the size and breadth of some ESOP companies. Just because a company is an ESOP doesn't mean that it can ignore the median pay and requirements for a particular role it is looking to fill. In fact, according to the 2024 ESOP Executive and Director Compensation Survey from the National Center for Employee Ownership,[32] 29% to 40% of respondents used stock-based compensation for their executive team (the range provided accounts for variation in executive positions).

Because there is flexibility in what proportion of a company is ESOP-owned, there's also flexibility in how the executive team is compensated.

[31] "COLA increases for dollar limitations on benefits and contributions," IRS, irs.gov, updated August 26, 2025, https://www.irs.gov/retirement-plans/cola-increases-for-dollar-limitations-on-benefits-and-contributions#:~:text=The%20tax%20law%20places%20limits%20on%20the,(IRA%2C%20401(k)%2C%20SEP%2C%20SIMPLE%20IRA%2C%20403(b)%2C%20457(b)%2C.

[32] National Center for Employee Ownership, "Report on the 2024 ESOP Compensation Survey" (PDF), NCEO, November 2024.

While part of their compensation is still going to be ESOP shares, there will likely need to be some additional equity compensation and bonus plans on the table as well to ensure senior management talent aligns with the complexity of the organization. An ESOP structure creates many tools in the toolbox.

There's an opportunity to allocate various types of synthetic equity within an ESOP. Synthetic equity doesn't involve the allocation of actual company stock but is, in essence, a bonus that mirrors the share price. One type of synthetic equity that is fairly common for ESOP companies is a stock appreciation rights plan (or SAR plan). Let's say an executive receives a SAR award when the share price is $100. Their bonus then becomes tied to how much the share price increases (or decreases) relative to that amount. After the specified period of time, they receive a cash bonus that is tied to the value of the shares. So if an executive entered the plan when the stock was valued at $100 per share and ended the specified time period with 2,500 fully vested SARs when the share price was $150, the executive would get a cash bonus of $125,000 (2,500 SARs times $50 of growth per SAR). Because it is a bonus, the flexibility is endless.

The benefit to the company of allocating synthetic equity is that there's no cash outflow at the time of the award. This is not the case when true equity shares are allocated. The benefit to the participant of receiving synthetic equity is that there is no current tax implication; however, when the award is paid, it is taxed as ordinary income, rather than at the capital gains rate[33] since it is considered a compensation expense. Who pays the taxes is ultimately determined by how this program is structured.

Similar to the ESOP, synthetic equity does still follow a vesting schedule. However, as you may have guessed, there is flexibility in how the company sets up its vesting plan for synthetic equity.

Another form of executive compensation available is allocation of management units of stock. While we use this for executives already on our team, this is particularly valuable to us when we are making

[33] "Phantom Stock and Stock Appreciation Rights (SARs)," National Center for Employee Ownership, nceo.org, accessed October 31, 2025, https://www.nceo.org/articles/phantom-stock-appreciation-rights-sars.

acquisitions because this allows for the former owners to have rollover equity in HB Global. During the acquisition, we allow the exiting owner to take on debt or equity in our company. If they choose equity, the owner receives some of the sale proceeds in the form of management units which, in essence, allows them to defer taxes and be engaged in HB Global as a whole.

You can think of the tax difference in management units as compared to synthetic equity like the difference between a regular IRA and a Roth IRA. When it comes to synthetic equity, there is no cash outflow when the program is set up. The total value of the gain is paid out at the end of the program, but it's taxed as ordinary income. For management units, this is real equity ownership which is purchased up front, so we're loaning post-tax dollars on the front-end, and then this income is taxed at capital gains rates on the back end. So for management units, there's a cash outlay at the beginning but better tax treatment later, and for synthetic equity there's no cash outlay at the beginning but a less favorable tax treatment to the recipient later at the time of the cash payment.

For a growth company, not having the cash outflow early is important. However, management units also make it easier to raise capital because it gives us more flexibility in raising additional capital through issuing additional equity or debt. There's no right or wrong answer, but you can align this with your strategy. We are a capital consumer and have aligned our strategy accordingly by utilizing management units as a form of alignment.

Aside from these common areas of executive compensation, there are various levers to pull for potential flexibility, such as how K-1s are handled, and many other considerations. You already know what I'm going to say next.

It's important to consult with an ESOP and tax advisor on these matters. While there is immense flexibility, there are also many guidelines and regulations as it relates to the IRS, ERISA (Employee Retirement Income Security Act of 1974), ESOP guidelines, and more. I'm just a guy who happened into ESOP as a practical solution in the recession that aligned with my personal goals for the company. Use my thoughts to brainstorm, but consult with an expert before taking action.

Speed of Buyback

There's another major consideration as it relates to compensation: speed of buyback and distributions. This decision impacts current and former employee owners. If an employee retires and is of retirement age, the company is required to start the buyback of shares beginning the following plan year. The company has to make payments at least annually and can take no more than five years to buy back the shares. If the employee leaves the company and is not of retirement age, the company is required to start the buyback of shares beginning no later than six years after the plan year that the employee left, and the company has five years to buy back all shares. The pre-determined retirement age can be plan specific but cannot be later than age 65 with five years of service. Companies may buy back shares in a lump sum right away or may buy back the shares over the whole five-year period, and they are able to choose any options in between (i.e. buy the shares back over three years).[34]

> **Technical Note:** The five-year period that distributions must be completed over can be extended for larger balances that are indexed over $1,415,000 at the time of this writing.[35]

At HB Global, we execute using the entirety of the five years that is allowed to buy back the shares of a former employee owner. Once an employee owner hits retirement age, we buy back the shares in equal installments over five years. We also have a provision in our plan that allows for early retirement. If an employee owner opts for retirement before age 59 ½, we buy back the shares between years six and ten.

[34] "When Will I Be Paid? The ESOP Participant's Guide to ESOP Distribution Rules," National Center for Employee Ownership, nceo.org, accessed October 31, 2025, https://www.nceo.org/articles/how-esop-distributions-work-for-esop-participants-rules-and-guidance.

[35] Corey Rosen, "IRS Announces 2025 COLA Plan Limits," *Employee Ownership Blog*, National Center for Employee Ownership, nceo.org, November 15, 2024, https://www.nceo.org/employee-ownership-blog/irs-announces-2025-cola-plan-limits#:~:text=On%20November%201%2C%20the%20IRS,increases%20from%20$275%2C000%20to%20$280%2C000.

We elect this option because we're a growth company. We want to keep as much free cash flow as we can to invest in expanding and scaling our company. By buying back shares over a longer period, we are spending fewer resources on share repurchases and circulation and are instead utilizing those resources to invest back into the growth of the company.

When we acquired BBEC, they had actually been electing to buy back shares as quickly as possible, meaning all shares were bought back in a lump sum at the share price that was determined for that plan year when the employment ended. Often this buyback takes place several months after the conclusion of the plan year so the valuation can be completed and other logistics can be completed. When they were acquired, their company became subject to our plan design and share buyback plan.

> **Technical Note:** The speed at which a company buys back shares is dependent on plan design.

With this structure in place, employees that leave or retire from the company still benefit from (or are penalized for) the performance of the company even after their departure. It actually bothers some of our employees that former employees who work for competitors still see gains from the work they do. But these same employee owners will reap the rewards from the work of future employees when they retire or leave the company. Personally, I don't view it this way, as I just see us as a capital provider.

Employees also benefit indirectly from a slower buyback by us reinvesting the capital to grow the company rather than repurchase stocks. As the company grows, more value is created that will then positively impact their ESOP accounts.

A company that is more focused on maintaining its size and scope may elect to buy back shares right away. Instead of deploying capital and resources into growth, they use those resources to buy back shares as soon as employees retire. In this case, the shares are bought back right away and then subsequently allocated to existing employees. Current employees then receive more shares and retired employees receive their distributions without delay. This does, however, create a higher churn within the plan and utilizes more capital and resources. Retired employees also don't see any benefit or penalty for the success of the company after their retirement.

There are arguments for each philosophy as it relates to share repurchases. We elect to take the longest possible option to help fund our growth. Others may argue for the shortest possible option. And while we discussed the two extreme situations, companies may elect any option in between.

Speed of Share Allocation

As it relates to how cash ultimately gets distributed to employee owners, there is again flexibility in how companies can set this up. However, there are standard guidelines that must be followed. There are various ways to obtain and set up loans within these standards, which will create a framework for how quickly the shares are allocated. There are also regulations as to the speed at which shares can be allocated. I'll spare you the details of those regulations and specifications and will instead refer you to chat with a professional in this field who deals in ESOPs for a living.

What I will speak to is a few examples of how these allocations can take place for you to get a feel for it. These will demonstrate the flexibility in how ESOPs can be structured and how allocations can be made. No ESOP is identical. We'll start by discussing HB Global as a case study, but I will warn you that we operate outside of the industry norms.

HB Global Case Study

When we initially started the ESOP, I tied the actual loan we had to buy the company to how quickly the shares would be allocated to employees.

Technical Note: The ESOP loan and the loan to buy the company do not need to be tied together. There are different ways to set up ESOP loans.

As we approached the upper bounds of what the regulations allow for allocations within a given year, we shifted to allocating 12% of each employee owner's pay per year until shares ran out. We'd also allocate any shares we'd repurchased during that time, so frequently, employee owners would end up receiving 13-14% of their pay in share allocations. (This is where we stray from the industry norms. In a typical ESOP, the allocation rate per year is 10% of total compensation.)[36]

Using this methodology, we distributed 100% of our shares by the 13th year. This is an abnormally quick timeframe for an ESOP to allocate all of its shares. Philosophically, I wanted to tie the allocation of the shares to the loan because it's my belief that the employees should actually get the benefit from what they're doing as soon as possible, rather than drawing out the share allocation. I'm passionate that employee owners should get their fair share of what's being created in real time.

Technical Note: The loan can be made for any reasonable period of time and can be paid off more quickly depending on the allocation methodology that is used. For more explanation and information on these possibilities, consult with someone who does this for a living rather than the CEO of a mechanical contracting company.

That being said, there are other philosophies out there. Taking a longer period of time to allocate the shares has administrative advantages that decrease the risk of repurchase issues and make the business more sustainable to manage. To me, those benefits didn't hold enough weight,

[36] "ESOP contributions as a percentage of payroll, most recent fiscal year," National Center for Employee Ownership, test.nceo.org, accessed October 31, 2025, https://test.nceo.org/hubfs/sites/default/files/2023-01/ESOP%20contributions%20as%20a%20percentage%20of%20payroll.pdf.

but I'm not here to tell you my way is the right way. I'm here to raise awareness of your options because different options may make sense in different scenarios.

The industry has been moving to longer and longer ESOP loans, which is the mechanism to allocate shares. Sometimes this is even happening over 40 years or even longer. This creates a situation where all shares are never fully distributed, which means the employees don't get the full benefit of ever owning the company.

The benefit of this strategy is that it lowers repurchase obligations. The downside is that the employee benefit is lower, and the total equity value of the firm is never really owned by the employees. I wanted the employees who did the work to buy the company to actually get the benefit. After we allocated all the shares, we recirculated the shares to the employees for the same reason. The employees that are creating the resources to buy back the shares are getting the benefit of the work they did over the previous year.

BBEC Case Study

We acquired BBEC in 2018. The unique part of this acquisition was that BBEC was already an ESOP before joining our family of brands. They had structured their ESOP in a way that was fairly aligned with the industry norms when they set it up in 2000, so we'll use their structure for demonstration purposes as well.

BBEC allocated 5% of their shares per year. This 5% was not at all tied to compensation. So, for quick math, let's say BBEC had 100,000 shares (I'm making up numbers here); they would allocate 5,000 shares per year. When BBEC set up the ESOP in 2000, their goal was to allocate all of the shares over 20 years. If the equity value increases faster than payroll then the benefit as a percentage of employees' pay increases over time. This is often the case because of the highly leveraged nature of most ESOP transactions.

Execution of Acquisitions

There's also flexibility when it comes to executing acquisitions. When completing an acquisition, the acquiring ESOP can choose to issue additional shares or maintain the existing share count. These decisions ultimately impact the share price as well.

Furthermore, the acquiring ESOP can choose how they issue shares to the newly acquired company. For example, at HB Global, we honor the prior years of service for employees at the business that just joined our company. If an employee had been at the acquired company for ten years, we consider them already fully vested. If they've been there for a couple of years, they're 20% vested. This is an election that we make, although there is flexibility in how this is handled.

And if you have a growth mindset, being an ESOP can potentially put you in a better position to be an acquirer. ESOPs have a lot to offer to sellers of businesses to ensure that employees are taken care of and that the seller is getting liquidity out of the sale. The optionality in acquisition targets as an ESOP potentially increases.

Governance

While we've dedicated this chapter to discussing the flexibility of an ESOP, it's also important to discuss the governance around this structure. Even with the immense flexibility, oversight is crucial. If a business owner decides to transition to an ESOP, they need to put in place a trustee, which can be internal or external, and a fiduciary board of directors. As a business owner who's considering transitioning to an ESOP, it's important to consider that this governance structure then becomes part of your decision-making process.

Anytime we have an important decision at HB Global, we ask ourselves if it's a trustee decision or a board decision. If we get advice from legal counsel that it's a trustee decision, we will seek their approval. If legal counsel determines that it's not a trustee decision, we will seek the approval of the board. Some decisions, such as our decision to move from being 100% ESOP-owned to 80% ESOP-owned, must be approved by both governing bodies.

The CEO of the company is accountable to the Board of Directors and the trustee. This may be a turnoff to some people, but for me, as the leader of the company, I didn't mind taking accountability for our results. It just seemed to make sense. Sure, the board could fire me, but my outlook is that if I'm performing well, that won't be an issue. Furthermore, while there is some loss of autonomy because of the oversight of the board and trustee, transitioning to an ESOP still allows you as the leader of the company to retain most of the autonomy as compared to selling to private equity or another company.

Having a board doesn't need to be a daunting thing. Chances are that you already have an advisory board before transitioning to an ESOP, and you can now transition that to a fiduciary board. If that's the case, you already have a relationship with these board members. Furthermore, as you're building your board, you build a board that has the expertise you think you need to help guide the company. For example, if you don't have a lot of banking experience, you may bring on a trusted member of your network who has banking experience.

And while we do seek the consent of the board for certain important decisions, a strong majority of decisions still reside with the executive team. The CEO's relationship with the board is really what they make of it. That being said, there are certain decisions that are required to go through the board by third parties, but generally, it's up to the leadership team to determine which decisions the board should consent to.

Warren Buffett would articulate that the most important job of the board is to select the CEO and be in a position to evaluate their performance.[37] This outlook demonstrates the level of autonomy that still remains with the leadership team within a company.

One additional consideration to make when it comes to ESOP governance is that the trustee will appoint members for the fiduciary board and vice versa. This doesn't mean, however, that the CEO is cut out of the process. For example, when I feel there is a new board member or trustee who would add value to our company, I go to the trustee

[37] Lawrence Cunningham, "Warren Buffett's 10 commandments for running a successful business," make it, cnbc.com, updated July 19, 2017, https://www.cnbc.com/2017/07/17/warren-buffetts-10-commandments-on-boardroom-power-and-success.html#:~:text=1.

or board and notify them that I'd like to recommend that person for election to the board of directors. If the trustee agrees, they will make that appointment to the board. While it's generally smooth sailing, there are potential impasses that may result if there are disagreements between the CEO, trustee, and the board. I would typically call those extreme cases, though.

Governance is set up to ensure the success and protection of all those within a company. While there are additional considerations to make and parties involved when it comes to important decisions, a significant amount of autonomy is maintained in the ESOP structure in conjunction with this governance.

Unwinding an ESOP

Another point to consider is that an ESOP can be unwound if it makes sense. In some cases, an ESOP can be totally unwound and sold to a third party. In this case, it's actually important to think of all the considerations you made before becoming an ESOP, such as your intention for your exit and what your priorities are for who the business is sold to. And just like the front end, advisors will be key to this process.

The more common case for unwinding is after a business begins the transition to an ESOP by first selling 30% – 40% to the ESOP. They may need to backtrack on this decision for whatever reason. Maybe financial performance had deteriorated, and an ESOP no longer made sense. Or maybe they didn't like having to be accountable to a fiduciary board. The ESOP can still be unwound at this point.

That being said, the big caveat here is that the trustee and other parts of the governance structure must be on board with any decision to unwind the ESOP. The responsibility of the trustee is to do what's in the best interest of the participants. A trustee will weigh in on whether unwinding the ESOP is in the best interest of the participants, and if it is, will also ensure that the ESOP portion of the business is sold for a high enough price that the participants are not harmed in the process.

On My Soapbox – Flexibility Catered to Goals

A huge reason I advocate for the use of ESOPs is the flexibility in how they can be set up based on what the leadership team is trying to accomplish. Each business has different priorities and different ways that they want to deploy their capital and develop their culture. The flexibility of an ESOP structure is inherently set up to accommodate that.

I'm a firm believer that businesses that are proficient at generating capital shouldn't just keep excess capital without utilizing it. The benefit of an ESOP is that it allows businesses to deploy capital in a variety of ways depending on their goals. The ability to determine the speed at which you buy back shares is a great example.

HB Global is a growth-minded company. So, for us, I believe it's the best option for us to buy back our shares as slowly as possible to deploy that capital into growth opportunities. While it delays cash being put into our retirees' and former employees' hands, I believe they ultimately receive more value in the long term from this approach because of the value that is created from our growth and acquisitions.

However, I think there are definitely arguments to buy back shares as quickly as possible, too. For companies that aren't looking to grow but are generating excess capital, I think deploying the capital to buy back shares right away is a great option. It's no different than a public company producing a lot of free cash flow and distributing it as a dividend back to shareholders.

The moral of the story is, if you have a particular goal, value, or impact that is important to you as a business owner, an ESOP can be set up in a way that facilitates your accomplishment of that. The bonus is that you are inherently taking care of your employees in the process by allowing them to share in that value creation.

Another Perspective – BBEC Employee Owners

Let's hear what some members of our BBEC subsidiary have to say about employee ownership, given their unique perspective of BBEC having been an ESOP since 2000.

> "As an original member of the BBEC Electrical Contractors ESOP program, I was unsure on how the process worked, but was told by the original owner that by just coming to work, giving my best, and sticking around a while (about 25 years) I'd be given a retirement plan without costing me a nickel out of pocket!
>
> "Jump ahead to 2018, we merged with HB McClure Company, another ESOP company with the same mentality 'Team, Grit and Growth,' which helped speed up the 'Growth.'
>
> "And today, in 2025, I'm weeks away from my retirement...it's amazing that Bob Whalen and our original owner (what, just one generation apart from each other...) had the same vision for success while keeping their employees involved for all to succeed!!"
>
> *Steven A. Lyons – Estimator*

> "As an employee of the BBEC division who has advanced from warehouse helper to operations in a little over a decade, it is safe to say that the organization focuses on prioritizing the growth and development of their team. Culture and focus built around the employees create endless opportunity that is difficult to find within a large organization.

"The ESOP opportunity given to the employees who join the HB Global team gives a level of future financial comfort most do not have."

Cody Bush – Field Operations Manager

"Working for an employee-owned company gives me a strong sense of ownership and accountability. Knowing that our shared goals and teamwork directly benefit not just us, but our families as well, motivates me to bring greater care, commitment, and effort to everything I do."

Nikki Lockard – Project Manager Assistant

"Working for an ESOP company creates value, not just for the company, but for all its employees by redistributing its earnings back to its employees. This builds trust, commitment, teamwork, and a sense of pride as your efforts directly contribute to the company's success and your own financial success."

Ryan Harman – Superintendent

Chapter 7
Creating a Win-Win-Win Scenario

When a business sells to an ESOP company, it creates a win-win-win situation. What do I mean by this? In this win-win-win scenario, the sellers get a win in what they're trying to accomplish, the employees of the buyer get a win in the value that's created for them, and the employees of the company being sold get wins in a variety of ways.

A unique case that demonstrates both the benefits of being an ESOP and the benefits of selling to an ESOP is our acquisition of BBEC. The leadership at BBEC at the time was looking to transition out and needed a solution for the future. HB Global had been in the same home market as BBEC, and we'd worked on many projects with them. We'd taken care of the plumbing and mechanical, while they'd taken care of the electrical. Because they were already an ESOP and we were an ESOP, the leadership team reached out to us. They wanted to make an exit but didn't have a plan in place. They proposed the acquisition of BBEC by HB Global, where HB Global would figure out the succession of the business.

We completed the acquisition and used some of our talent at HB Global to fill in the exiting leadership at BBEC. BBEC also immediately received the benefit of a premium being paid in the transaction, our balance sheet, diversification, management depth, and corporate infrastructure (IT, risk management, etc.).

But the benefits didn't just take place in the short-term; they've continued to compound over time through the ESOP program. As of this writing, there are several long-tenured BBEC employees who have crossed or are nearing the million-dollar ESOP balance threshold!

Let's look at a median employee as an example to really show the growth over the years. After HB Global acquired BBEC in 2018, this example employee had an account balance of $442,000. At the time, he was making $73,000 as a technician. This meant he had accumulated about six times his annual pay in retirement savings through the ESOP. This employee now makes about $80,000, and his ESOP account balance is $1.522 million as of September 30, 2024, with the HB Global share price at $164.40. That means he's accumulated about 20 times his annual pay in retirement savings through the ESOP, which is enough for him to maintain his standard of living in retirement.

While this acquisition benefited the employees at BBEC, it was also beneficial to HB Global and its employees in part because of the nature of an ESOP-to-ESOP acquisition. When this type of deal occurs, there is actually no cash exchanged. Instead, the merger is based on the value of the shares, and an exchange ratio is calculated. This creates a very efficient deal.

While this story is a unique case of an ESOP acquiring an already employee-owned company, it highlights how the seller and employees at both companies can win from an acquisition. Some of these wins are inherent in the ESOP structure itself, and some of these wins are dependent on the buyer and the fit between the buyer and seller.

Finding the Right Partner

While there are many advantages inherent to the ESOP structure, there are also other advantages dependent on who you sell to.

As a seller, you've hopefully spent a lot of time setting intentions for how you'd like to exit the business and what your priorities are for both yourself and your business upon exit. If you've decided that you'd like to exit to an ESOP, you can again put those intentions and priorities to use in determining who to sell to.

Your first decision will be whether to sell to an ESOP trust or sell to another ESOP company. When I transitioned HB McClure to an ESOP, I sold it to an ESOP trust. This allowed me to maintain relative control and autonomy in my leadership of the business, which was a priority for me.

That doesn't mean that's the only option for maintaining a certain level of control when selling your business. For example, our goal for the subsidiaries we acquire at HB Global is for those businesses to maintain a certain level of autonomy. Yes, we provide standards for them to work within and ultimately have the final say on things, but our goal is for them to maintain their brand and be able to have autonomy in how they go about their days.

The thought of having a relatively clean slate when selling to an ESOP trust may be appealing to some sellers, but there also may be aspects of an existing ESOP company that are appealing. For example, at HB Global, in addition to the ESOP plan, we also have a bonus structure in place that rewards employees for the performance of their subsidiaries each year. This is an advantage unique to us that a seller may consider.

When it comes down to it, it's most important for a seller to exit to an option that is aligned with their culture. We only acquire subsidiaries who are a cultural fit for our company because that's where win-win-win situations happen. In fact, before even talking about price or financials, we have a conversation on the culture and priorities of the business and owners at the outset of the acquisition process. It's important to us that the business already has their leadership succession talent embedded in the organization to ensure a smoother transition (this is something we've learned and have changed over time). We also look for sellers who want to maintain the legacy of their business and take care of the employees who helped get them to where they are today.

Not all sellers will share these priorities. But there will always be an option for a seller to exit that aligns with their goals and intentions. This could mean evaluating different ESOP companies, selling to an ESOP trust, or choosing a different sale option altogether.

A Win-Win-Win Success Story

Earlier, we discussed the win-win-win situation created through our acquisition of BBEC, which was already employee-owned. If you're reading this book, however, you likely aren't already structured as an ESOP, so let's take a look at another example of creating a win-win-win scenario in which we acquired a new subsidiary that had been family-owned.

In 2014, we acquired IT Landes, a mechanical contracting company in the Philadelphia area. It was our first major acquisition. Sure, we had completed some smaller acquisitions in our area of companies that were much smaller than us, but IT Landes was a completely different ballgame.

At the time, HB McClure was generating about $40 million in revenue, and IT Landes was generating about $25 million in revenue. HB McClure had about 200 employee owners, and IT Landes had about 100 employees. The two companies were, however, comparable in profitability because of the efficient profit margins at IT Landes.

IT Landes has been a successful acquisition for us. Their revenue has grown about three times since we acquired them, and their profitability has grown about 50-75%. While the profitability hasn't kept pace with the rate of increase in revenue, this was part of the strategy. IT Landes was an incredibly efficient profit generator when it was ⅓ of the size it is today. When we acquired IT Landes, we knew we'd lose some profit efficiency but that we could grow the profitability overall and create more value for the employees at both companies.

Today, IT Landes has about 200 employees and generates about $75 million in revenue. There is 50% more in the accounts of employees at the company than what the purchase price had been to the original owners. The business is thriving in the autonomy they've been able to keep accompanied with new resources and systems to empower that autonomy.

While IT Landes hasn't been our *most* successful acquisition as it relates to the return we've gotten from it, the ten years of history demonstrate how a win-win-win can grow over time. Let's talk about all the initial wins at the point of purchase that got us to where we are today to demonstrate this win-win-win concept.

Win for the Seller

Our promise to the Landes brothers when we entered discussions to purchase their company was that they could get the liquidity out of their business and ensure that their employees were taken care of even after they exited the business. We committed to continue their brand in that market and allow the business to operate with a fair level of autonomy.

They really bought into this as sellers because they'd seen a lot of businesses in their area that had been basically gutted by selling to private equity. They didn't want that for their employees or their brand. After all, the business had been going strong since 1929.

We didn't have a significant track record as an ESOP at that point, but they were willing to take the leap of faith with us. While there were some surface-level cultural differences, the foundational aspects of our culture were aligned, specifically our core value of trust. Trust was incredibly important to both sides, and IT Landes trusted in our commitment to them and their employees.

Selling to us also meant that the Landes brothers could exit the business relatively quickly. They were able to get their liquidity, and because of our proximity to their company, we'd be able to staff and handle the transition using their internal team and our team from Harrisburg as necessary. This was another win for them as sellers. These brothers had grown up with the business and had been working in it since they were 18 years old. They had operated the business as a partnership for 30 years and were basically just tired and wanted to sell.

An additional benefit to the sellers was that we were willing to enter into a 1042 transaction with them. This essentially meant that they could defer the capital gain taxes on the sale indefinitely if they met certain criteria in the transaction. This type of deal is far too technical for the scope of this book, but you can think of it similarly to a Section 1031 exchange (real estate transaction). For more information on 1042 transactions, consult an ESOP advisor or tax expert.

Win for the Employees of the Seller

A large constituency that wins when their company is sold to the ESOP is the employees, who are now employee owners of the company. With no action or contribution from their side, the employees of IT Landes automatically became employee owners of our business when we acquired them as an ESOP.

We've done many acquisitions since IT Landes, with varying degrees of buy-in from the employees of the seller. We were fortunate that for this first major acquisition, the Landes brothers had portrayed the sale very positively, and their team got a good bit of comfort from that.

Despite this comfort level, I think employees of acquired companies typically come in with a "show-me" attitude, which, by the way, I think is totally justified. While there is an initial level of skepticism, our employee ownership structure and the common core value of trust helped the employees at IT Landes to give us an initial benefit of the doubt.

That being said, being an ESOP isn't a magic bullet. It has its advantages to building trust, but we still had to put in the work to nurture this relationship and the trust associated with it.

Each morning, I'd wake up early and drive an hour and 45 minutes to IT Landes to help facilitate a smooth transition. I also wanted to ensure we honored the facets of the business that had made them most successful while helping them to get a little bit better each day. (As we scaled the roll-up model in later years, I was unable to be at new acquisitions day in and day out, but we'd learned lessons that taught us how to do this effectively.)

Building trust would happen over time as employee owners saw their ESOP balances grow, but we wanted to prove our trustworthiness in the short run as well. We did this by paying them higher-level bonuses than what they were accustomed to. The median pay has also increased 22% during our tenure with IT Landes (2014 to 2024).

Now, of the 47 employees at IT Landes in 2014 who were eligible to participate in the ESOP, 33 of those individuals are still with us today (as of 9/30/2024). Over those 10 years, they've amassed a median ESOP account balance of $265,000, and those 33 individuals have over 35% of the total IT Landes ESOP Value in their accounts.

Aside from monetary benefits, the employees benefited in intangible ways as well. After becoming part of HB McClure, IT Landes got access to new resources and processes that were available from our company. These new systems helped empower employees to have increased levels of autonomy through the availability of information. Furthermore, while not required as an ESOP, we practice open book management to foster trust and transparency with employees, where they have access to financial information related to their business. This created an environment of increased accountability where insightful questions began to bubble up from employees genuinely invested in the success of their company.

Win for the Employees of the Buyer

When we acquired IT Landes, there were mixed emotions from the employees at HB McClure. On one hand, there was a sense of general excitement. Our team knew that this would lead to new growth and new opportunities. There was also a hope of increased value creation.

On the other hand, there was a certain level of apprehension. This was our first major acquisition. It meant significantly increasing our size through a complex transaction only a few years after becoming an ESOP. Because our business was employee-owned, our employees knew that their success now depended on the success of this acquisition and the value that this new company could also help to create.

Much of this apprehension came from risk aversion and the tendency of folks to only think about the downside of risk (a topic I'm very passionate about but won't dive into *quite yet*). In my mind, however, there was incredible upside potential of the value we could create for our existing employees as well.

There were definitely some growing pains, especially considering how close the two companies were geographically, because the success of the individual employees was tied to the success of the overall entity as a whole. Now, despite these initial pains, there's never been a better environment for cooperation between the two.

In time, our employees saw how this growth positively impacted them. Now our employees have been part of several acquisitions and have seen how each new acquisition has generally led to increased value in their accounts and new growth opportunities. When we announce acquisitions today, there is a level of palpable positive buzz and excitement that we've grown into over time as we've built trust with our employees.

A Bonus Win for the Buyer

As a buyer, there is a fourth win that can take place in an ESOP transaction, depending on the nature of the transaction. Overall, in addition to the many tangible benefits to our employees, there are benefits to the company as a whole that create value in the long run. Some of the major benefits we see are geographic diversification, diversification in our end-user base (i.e. entering new service markets), and acquiring talented employees.

Because we acquired IT Landes, we were able to enter a new geographic market. Although Harrisburg and Philadelphia are not far from each other, their markets look different and don't always move in lockstep. As we've completed more acquisitions and realized our ability to scale, we've been able to expand across the US and even internationally.

IT Landes also allowed us to serve a more diverse end-user base. They had a significant portfolio in senior care, which was not a niche that we had typically served. As we've grown over time, we've been able to grow the end users that we serve.

All this diversification pays off for our employees because different markets and end users see different economic cycles. While one region of the US or industry may see a downturn, our subsidiaries in different markets can help us to maintain our success overall and take care of our employee owners. For us specifically, construction is a lagging indicator of a recession, so the effects are shown at different points depending on how the business is structured. You can see how this plays out with some of our subsidiaries in the chart on the next page. Even during a challenging economic environment, a representative mix of our subsidiaries would have remained profitable overall if they were all part of HB Global at that time.

Acquisitions also lead us to bring on many new, talented individuals onto our teams. And the more we've grown, the more we've been able to nurture this talent through new educational programs, stretch assignments, and overall opportunities.

On My Soapbox – The Two Tails of Risk

People tend to view risk as a one-sided tail. They're constantly focused on what can go wrong and not also focused on how things can go right, or even better than expected. The apprehension of our employees when we made our first big acquisition demonstrates this. There was worry about what could go wrong, but since that time, so much has gone right. Because of this evidence towards the positive, our employees are now very energized when we make acquisitions. They have a much different perspective on risk than when we first started this strategy.

Operating Profit		Recession								
Subsidiary	2007	2008	2009	2010	2011	2012	2013	2014	2015	2016
Subsidiary 1	$1,018,747	$2,194,642	$1,144,561	$1,084,531	$1,649,736	$2,290,302	$3,832,883	$2,493,682	$4,085,720	$5,137,393
Subsidiary 2	$772,000	$2,016,000	$4,306,000	$213,000	$764,000	$2,834,000	$2,671,000	$1,399,597	$3,013,897	$3,723,998
Subsidiary 3	$3,072,571	$1,606,065	($240,474)	$222,361	$540,924	$619,797	$624,144	$1,180,718	$2,399,017	$1,841,030
Subsidiary 4	$1,812,249	$2,714,240	$4,177,647	$3,337,918	($704,365)	($2,665,823)	($963,413)	$779,806	($2,649,976)	$851,537
Subsidiary 5	$928,898	$2,011,648	($310,407)	$66,653	$119,451	$328,862	$788,953	$1,204,882	$2,170,010	$2,032,351
Subsidiary 6	$509,643	$200,673	$284,910	$292,958	$291,058	$218,811	($143,749)	($2,570)	$218,603	$1,039,865
Total	$ 8,114,108	$ 10,743,268	$ 9,362,237	$ 5,217,421	$ 2,660,804	$ 3,625,949	$ 6,809,818	$ 7,056,115	$ 9,237,271	$ 14,626,174

Don't get me wrong, you don't want to always just look at the bright side of everything in business. It's important to consider the downsides of risk, but to overlook the upside of risk would be a lapse in judgment. If we had not taken on the risk of acquisitions, we wouldn't be who we are today. We wouldn't be geographically diversified. We wouldn't be diversified in our end users. We wouldn't have acquired masses of talented employees. We wouldn't have been able to make as big of an investment in employee education. We wouldn't have been able to create as many new opportunities or stretch assignments for our employees. The list could go on and on.

HB Global is a great example to show both sides of risk. By the end of 2024, we had 12 subsidiaries because of the acquisition moves that we've made. Many of those have turned out very well. Several of our subsidiaries have even created more value than expected. The chart on the next page demonstrates the two tails of risk. For our subsidiaries that have been around long enough, you can see their return on invested capital (ROIC) for the first five years after acquisition. Our target is 23%. You can see that most of our acquisitions have met or exceeded that goal. Yes, there was one acquisition that did not pan out as expected. That's part of taking risk. Yes, there will be downside, but we've also seen immense upside. Despite the acquisition that did not work out, our weighted average return on invested capital is still 34%, which significantly exceeds our goal of 23%. When the risks we take don't work out, we use them as opportunities to learn. We don't just decide to become risk averse.

Debt is another great example of the two tails of risk and the potential upsides of taking on that risk. Imagine how different our economy would look today if people didn't have access to mortgages. According to the Federal Reserve Economic Data, home ownership in the US was 65.7% at the end of 2024.[38] How much of that would be possible if people were required to pay cash?

Debt exemplifies how viewing risk through the long-term view helps illuminate both the potential upside and the potential downside of the risk. Mortgages are typically 30 years. We view our home purchases

[38] "Homeownership Rate in the United States," FRED, fred.stlouisfed.org, updated July 28, 2025, https://fred.stlouisfed.org/series/RHORUSQ156N.

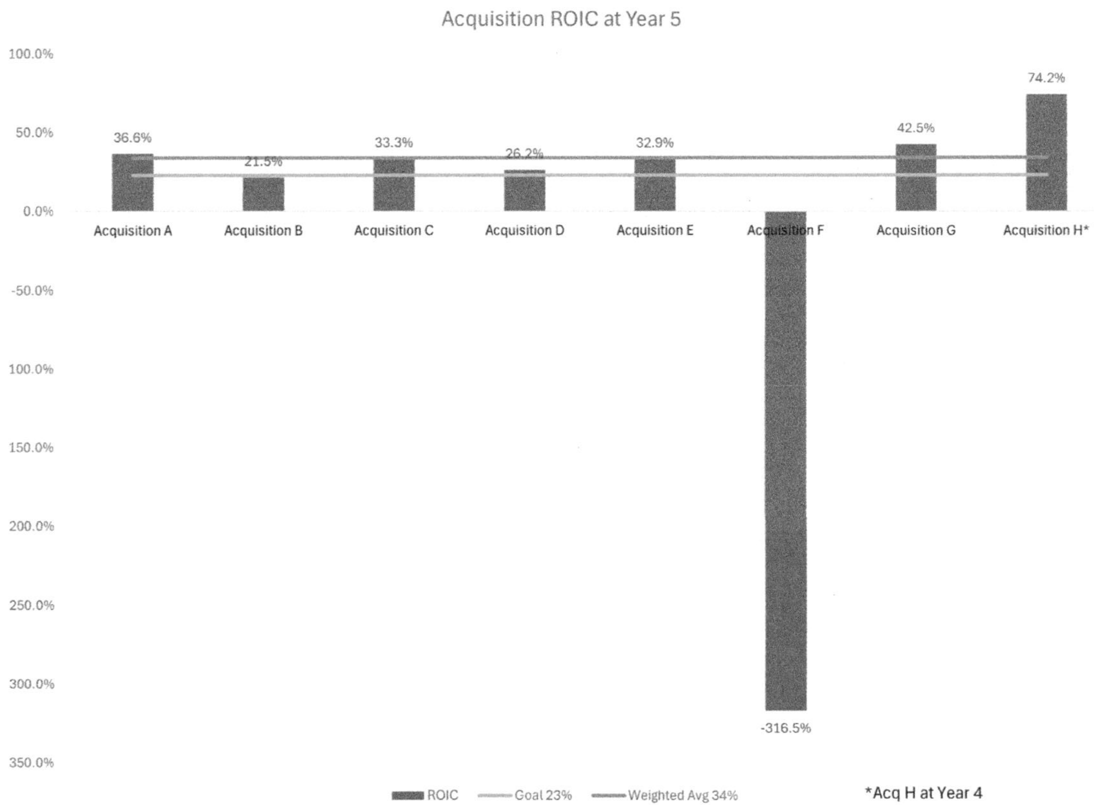
Acquisition ROIC at Year 5
100.0%
50.0%
0.0%
-50.0%
100.0%
150.0%
200.0%
250.0%
300.0%
350.0%
36.6%
21.5%
33.3%
26.2%
32.9%
-316.5%
42.5%
74.2%
Acquisition A
Acquisition B
Acquisition C
Acquisition D
Acquisition E
Acquisition F
Acquisition G
Acquisition H*
ROIC
Goal 23%
Weighted Avg 34%
*Acq H at Year 4

as an investment that we can pay off over time and that we wouldn't typically otherwise be able to make with cash. Take on too much debt, though, and you could find yourself underwater. The same thing applies with business debt.

Some business owners view debt as a bad thing, but taking on the appropriate amount of leverage has allowed us to grow as a company to where we are today. We absolutely could not have purchased IT Landes without debt. We hadn't created enough free cash flow or the resources on our balance sheet that we have now. However, becoming too highly levered would put too much stress on the business. It's a balancing act.

It's always important when assessing the two tails of risk to consider what is the appropriate level of risk to take given the situation. As HB Global has grown, our risk profile and tolerance have changed over that time. The same level of risk that we took on in our earlier years is no longer appropriate for us to take on now. When we first paid out $600 in allocations to our employees' ESOP accounts, taking more risk to create value made a lot more sense. But now we have people who can fund their full retirement with the ESOP balances. Take the median balance of employee owners who have been with us since we became an ESOP 14 years ago. They now have a median balance of $392,000 in their account. As a company, we certainly don't want to put that balance at risk, and individual employee owners certainly don't want us putting that at risk because that balance could fund their entire retirement when invested wisely.

A big part of risk-taking is value judgment. For example, I paid off my house as soon as I could. Given the interest rate on my mortgage, it may not have been the best financial move. I could've put that money into other vehicles that had a higher rate of return. But paying off the mortgage sooner rather than later gave me peace of mind in an area of my life where I'd prefer not to have the risk. I do, however, take other financial risks in my life, like how much of my net worth is concentrated in HB Global.

No matter your appetite for risk, it's important to keep in mind that there's always a potential upside in addition to the potential downside. Keeping both in mind helps you to make a sound decision that is aligned with your values and intentions.

Another Perspective – Chris Landes

Let's hear from Chris Landes, former owner of IT Landes, who decided to sell his company to HB Global in 2014.

1. What were your priorities when selling your company?

> Obtaining market value for the company along with ensuring growth and prosperity for the company and its employees after the transition.

2. How did it feel selling your company to an ESOP?

> After understanding what an ESOP was it became clear it was the perfect fit!

3. How would you describe the success and legacy of your business today?

> I couldn't be more proud of our decision and humble enough to acknowledge the company has grown and been more successful for our employees and the industry after becoming an ESOP.

Chapter 8
Creating Alpha

For those familiar with the investing world, you've likely heard of the term alpha. Most people think of alpha as the return money managers can create over and above what is the expected level of return relative to the risk involved. Investopedia defines alpha as "a term used in investing to describe an investment strategy's ability to beat the market, or its 'edge.' Alpha is thus also often referred to as excess return or the abnormal rate of return in relation to a benchmark when adjusted for risk."[39]

[39] James Chen, "Understanding Alpha in Investing: Definition and Examples," Investopedia, updated October 7, 2025, https://www.investopedia.com/terms/a/alpha.asp#:~:text=Alpha%20(α)%20is%20a%20term,benchmark%2C%20when%20adjusted%20for%20risk.

An easy way to think about it is to consider it like this: if you're investing in large public company stocks, your alpha is the return you get over and above what the S&P 500 returns. If the S&P 500 return is 10% and your return was 12%, you would have generated 2% alpha for that year. If you create alpha on a relatively consistent basis over most years, it starts to make a real difference. While 2% may not sound like much, it makes a big impact as this compounds over a long period of time. It's the inverse of the impact of investing fees. If you have to pay a 1% fee, that 1% ends up being a big chunk of change as you miss out on the potential for that to compound over time.

As I evolved into the view that my professional mission was focused on the return I could get for the employees at HB Global, I started to think about what alpha looks like in our business and in ESOPs as a whole. The most direct analysis of how successful I am at my job is the alpha that we create for the employees of HB Global compared to what they would gain working with somebody else.

A Rough Example

Using data ranging from 2010 to 2020, we compared ourselves to the companies in the Russell 1000. I'll admit, this was not the right comparison group. For those unfamiliar, Morningstar explains that the Russell 1000 "includes approximately 1000 of the largest securities based on a combination of their market cap and current index membership."[40] We were only a $25 million company in 2010, and even at our largest during that decade, we only grew to a few hundred million dollars. However, we were still curious to perform this analysis to ensure we were giving our employees a great return in their retirement accounts.

When comparing our returns to the companies on the Russell 1000, we would've been the number 3 returning stock on the index. In that decade, there would've only been two companies that outperformed us.

We take a lot of pride in that because that means our employees would've had a hard time finding a better investment than us during

[40] "Russell 1000 PR USD," MorningStar.com, accessed October 31, 2025, https://www.morningstar.com/indexes/ixus/rui/quote.

that decade. Because of our employee ownership structure, they are heavily invested in us since their ESOP accounts contain our shares, making them tied to the performance of the company and our share price.

This demonstrates the immense alpha that I believe we are generating for our employees and the alpha that I believe ESOPs as a whole generate as businesses and for their employees.

How ESOPs Generate Alpha for Employee Owners

I believe that ESOPs are consistently producing alpha for our employees. It starts by looking at compensation and benefits. If a company is paying market-based compensation and benefits, they are generating zero alpha. To generate alpha, we need to create value for employees over and above this market-based pay and benefits.

According to Fidelity, employers can vary in their 401(k) match programs, but "a common setup is for employers to contribute $1 for every $1 an employee contributes up to 3% of their salary, then 50 cents on the dollar for the next 2% of an employee's salary." This would equate to a 4% match if an employee contributes 5% of their salary. The Fidelity data shows that the overall average match was 4.8% in June 2024. This is skewed higher than the 4% of a common plan because of plans that offer higher match rates.[41]

According to Investopedia, participants in 401(k) plans administered by Vanguard earned a 9.7% average annual return and a median annual return of 10.4% for the five years ending 2023.[42] This means that if all other compensation and benefits are on par with the market, anything we produce as an ESOP above this return is considered alpha.

[41] "How does a 401(k) match work?" Fidelity, fidelity.com, June 30, 2025, https://www.fidelity.com/learning-center/smart-money/average-401k-match.

[42] Adam Hayes, "What Are the Average 401(k) Returns? See How Yours Compare," Investopedia.com, January 28, 2025, https://www.investopedia.com/401-k-returns-and-how-they-compare-to-others-8779625#:~:text=Average%2FMedian%20401(k)%20Returns,-In%20recent%20years&text=7%20Looking%20at%20longer%2Dterm,return%20(median%2C%209.2%25).

Let's take another perspective and look at HB Global as an example relative to the stock market. We make a conscious effort to ensure that the value we create meets or exceeds that of the market. Over our 14-year history, we've generated a 33% return on our stock. In the chart on the following page, you can see this compared to the S&P 500, which had an average annual rate of return of 15%.

Within the last couple of years, we've started making a 401(k) grant where we contribute 3% of each employee owner's base pay to their 401(k) account. Because we do this and meet or exceed market for compensation and other benefits, most of the value the ESOP produces for our employee owners is alpha – over and above what they would generally receive in the market working in a similar industry and business.

I believe this to be true for most – if not all – ESOPs because it's important for an ESOP to meet market level for factors outside of ESOP contributions. If a company isn't meeting the market for compensation or benefits and relies too heavily on ESOP contributions, they aren't really taking care of their employees because employees also need to be taken care of in the here and now.

This notion that ESOPs as a whole are set up to produce alpha is supported by data points published by the NCEO in a 2021 report titled *S Corporation ESOPs: Advantages in an Uncertain Economy.* Data in this report shows that the median ESOP account balance was $80,500 while the median 401(k) balance was $30,000. The report also states that most S Corporation ESOPs were offering 401(k) in addition to ESOP contributions.[43]

Furthermore, a study by Ernst & Young showed that on average, the compound annual growth rate for an ESOP participant in an S-Corporation ESOP was 12.1%, which was about a third higher than what the S&P 500 showed for returns over the same time period.[44]

[43] "S Corporation ESOPs" (PDF), National Center for Employee Ownership, esca.us, June 2023, https://esca.us/wp-content/uploads/2023/07/NCEO-report-FINAL.pdf.

[44] Corey Rosen, "EY Study Shows ESOP Participants Fare Much Better," *Employee Ownership Blog,* nceo.org, May 16, 2022, https://www.nceo.org/employee-ownership-blog/ey-study-shows-esop-participants-fare-much-better.

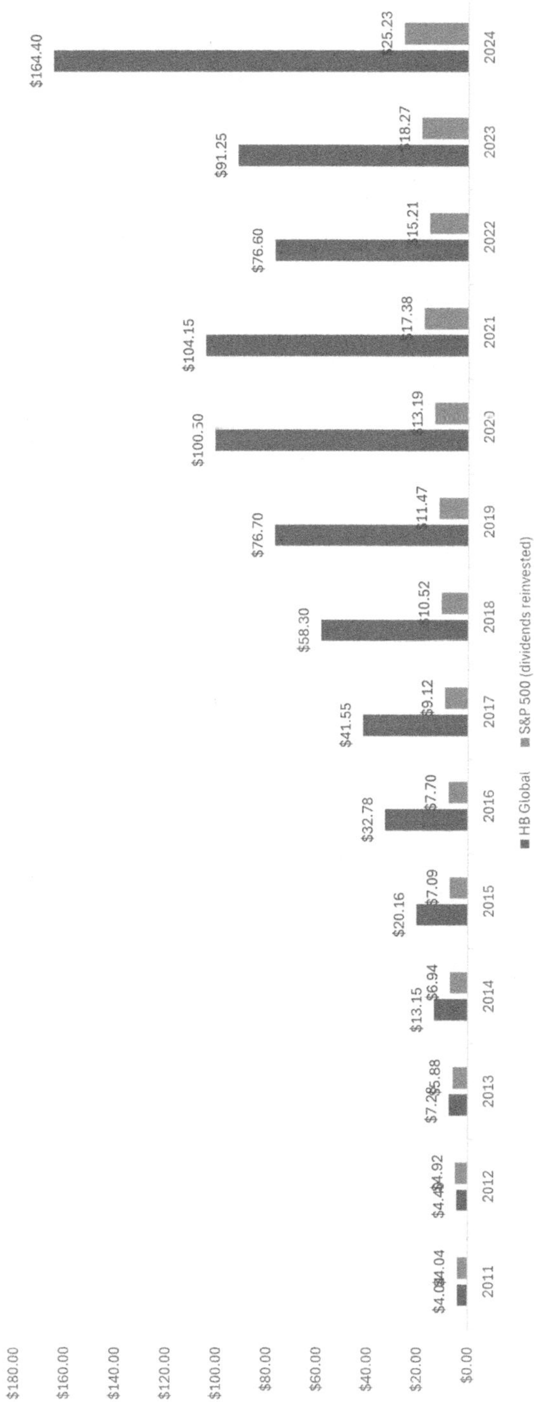
Share Price
HB Global
S&P 500 (dividends reinvested)
$180.00
$160.00
$140.00
$120.00
$100.00
$80.00
$60.00
$40.00
$20.00
$0.00
2011
2012
2013
2014
2015
2016
2017
2018
2019
2020
2021
2022
2023
2024
$164.40
$25.23
$91.25
$18.27
$76.60
$15.21
$104.15
$17.38
$100.30
$13.19
$76.70
$11.47
$58.30
$10.52
$41.55
$9.12
$32.78
$7.70
$20.16
$7.09
$13.15
$6.94
$5.88
$4.92
$4.04

You may also generate alpha by paying more than the market. We try to accomplish alpha in this area as well through our bonus programs. While our intent is to at least match the market on base pay, we exceed the market in what we pay out in bonuses.

That being said, alpha is all in the eyes of the beholder. There is a value judgment that takes place on the part of the employee as well. Maybe they'd rather receive more cash compensation in their base pay and worry less about saving for retirement. Let's face it, everyone has immediate needs to be addressed. That's where the intention of the employee comes in. Do they find value in the mission, benefits, and culture of an ESOP or do they find value elsewhere?

If their value system is aligned with that of what an ESOP can provide, then there's a strong chance an ESOP is going to produce alpha for them as it relates to the benefits they receive relative to being employed elsewhere in the market for their industry.

How ESOPs Generate Alpha for the Business

I believe the alpha that is generated is inherent in the ESOP structure. It is the business generating alpha as a whole that creates the value for the business to pass on to employees. In my mind, there are three key components that generate alpha for an ESOP: employees who are highly aligned, tax savings, and management decisions.

When employees are highly aligned with a company, they should be producing better results. When individuals are working towards the same goals as the overall company, there is increased motivation and greater incentive to perform. While possible in any business structure, this is quite difficult to achieve outside of an ESOP but can be easier in an ESOP.

The tax structure of an ESOP also generates alpha. If the business were not an ESOP, it would be subject as a company to pay whatever the marginal tax rate is for that business. As an ESOP, we no longer have to pay those income taxes for the percentage of the company that is ESOP-owned, and so we expand the pie that can be shared with employees by that much.

The third component is the decisions of management. These decisions will always impact alpha, but the catch here is that these can move alpha in either direction. The good news is that many of the cultural aspects of an ESOP naturally help leaders to make decisions in alignment with that mission and culture, which helps to increase alpha. However, if the management team isn't delivering on commitments aligned with the mission of an ESOP, they have the potential to deteriorate alpha. An ESOP shouldn't be considered the quick, guaranteed fix for culture or returns.

Impacts to returns due to management decision-making will be present in any business. An ESOP structure, however, naturally lends itself to producing alpha through the culture it encourages, the resulting employee alignment, and the tax savings. Furthermore, ESOPs typically outperform similar non-ESOP businesses. According to the NCEO in *An Introduction to ESOPs* by Scott Rodrick, employee-owned companies that utilize participative management typically grow 6% to 11% per year faster than would typically be expected.[45]

It's Not Just Us – WinCo Foods

We've talked a lot about how we can generate alpha, but WinCo Foods is another great example of this. WinCo Foods has about 140 employee-owned stores with over 20,000 employees. They were founded in 1967 in Boise, ID and became employee-owned in 1985.[46]

According to the NCEO, WinCo was the 2nd largest majority employee-owned company in the United States as of November 2024.[47] WinCo allocates shares annually at a rate of 20% of base pay. They also offer comprehensive health benefits, a 401(k) program in addition to the ESOP, help with tuition, and an Employee Assistance Program.[48]

[45] Scott Rodrick, An Introduction to ESOPs (National Center for Employee Ownership, 2025): 33.

[46] "About Us," WinCo Foods, wincofoods.com, accessed October 31, 2025, https://www.wincofoods.com/about-us.

[47] "The Employee Ownership 100," The National Center for Employee Ownership, nceo.org, updated October 2025, https://www.nceo.org/research/employee-ownership-100-largest-employee-owned-companies.

[48] "Join our Winning Team at WinCo Foods," careers.wincofoods.com, accessed October 31, 2025, https://careers.wincofoods.com/?q-about%2Fcareers%2F.

According to their website, if an employee owner had been part of their ESOP for the past ten years and received $5,000 in shares each year, the employee owner would now have an ESOP balance of almost $91,000.[49] This implies an approximately 12% return. Because WinCo also has a 401(k) program, we can assume that most, if not all, of this 12% return is alpha generated for employee owners.

ESOP Value as a Form of Measurement

Public companies have their stock valued in real time. Private companies don't have the benefit of seeing that. Many private companies don't even receive valuations for their businesses until it's time to transition ownership of the business. ESOPs are different because they are required to be valued every year.

Because ESOPs are valued every year, it's not only easy to track the alpha generated for the business and employees, but it also helps leadership to see the overall value that is created over time. We're able to see the enterprise value that we've created over the years and the value that's been added to the ESOP accounts as it relates to that. This is a fantastic measurement tool that goes above and beyond what owners can see simply by analyzing profit and loss statements. By receiving an annual valuation, ESOPs can see the true value of the company that's been created, which is directly influenced by the results and projections of the company. Of course, there are some assumptions built into the valuation, but overall, the valuation provides a great scorecard.

This scorecard gives leadership an excellent frame of reference. While goals aren't directly set related to this scorecard, it gives great feedback of how the company is doing to accomplish its goals and mission. It's no different than a score in a sports competition. There are more detailed strategy and goals within the game, but that strategy is informed by the score.

And it's not just the valuation number itself that gives great feedback to ESOP companies but also the ability to see how employee ESOP

[49] "WinCo Foods is proud to be employee-owned . . .," WinCo Foods, wincofoods.com, accessed October 31, 2025, https://www.wincofoods.com/employee-owned.

account balances are growing. Each year, I get a spreadsheet where I can see the value in every single employee's ESOP account, and every year, this day feels like Christmas morning to me. I get so excited to see the value that we've been able to create and directly share with our employees who played such a key role in getting us there.

Financials are a great tool to track the progress of a company, but the mechanism by which ESOPs receive a true valuation of the company takes that scorecard to a whole new level.

On My Soapbox – Worry over Repurchase Obligation

If ESOPs are structured in a way that they are able to produce alpha for the business as a whole and for employees more easily than other business structures, why are ESOPs not more prevalent? A major driver of this is worry over repurchase obligations. While new ESOPs have entered the market, others have sold to strategic buyers or other buyers to exit the ESOP and alleviate this concern. I think if we took a more rational view on repurchase obligations, ESOPs would still be growing. In fact, this is such a pervasive worry for those in the ESOP community and those interested in selling to an ESOP that a talk I gave on this topic in 2024 was standing room only.

So, what is repurchase obligation?

Repurchase obligation is buying back shares from former employees. The ESOP legislation gives you the first ten years where very little repurchase needs to happen. So you have a ten-year period to buy the initial company from the former owner without having to think about a substantial repurchase obligation. But after the ten-year mark, in some way, you're buying back the shares of former employees.

While there is so much worry about repurchase obligation in the ESOP community, there are three main arguments I make as to why repurchase obligation shouldn't be such a hindrance to the growth of ESOPs.

Transitions are Traumatic

It's always traumatic for a business to go through an ownership transition. Take a family business, for example. You may assume that because the business is being kept in the family that the transition will be more seamless, but there still needs to be a huge transition from one generation to the next. The next generation needs to actually purchase the business from the current ownership generation. This can create quite a bit of turmoil both in the business and in the family.

ESOPS, however, are systematic. To the extent you treat your employees well and your employees stay working for you, the transition happens over a fairly long period of time. At HB Global, we were trying to purchase the company as quickly as we could (within the bounds of regulations) to get that value in the hands of employees. It still took 13 years for 100% of the shares to be allocated to employees, as we paid down the loan we took out to become an ESOP.

So, in my view, I don't see how a business transition that takes place over a generation which then turns into systematic distributions, as is the case with ESOPs, can be more worrisome or traumatic than a large transaction that takes place once a generation to transition ownership.

Really, there are only a few options where there isn't this sort of massive undertaking of a transition. One example is a public company because they have no obligation to buy back the equity. Another example is partnerships structured similarly to an accounting firm or a legal firm, which have a natural mechanism to continue transitioning ownership. But unless this type of transition mechanism is built into your structure, you basically decide between large, once-in-a-generation transitions or a systematic repurchase process each year in an ESOP.

Tax Savings

One of the advantages we've continually talked about is the tax savings from structuring your business as an ESOP. I believe that, in essence, the tax savings that you get are very close to the proximity of what you're going to have to repurchase. Therefore, the tax savings may help fund your repurchases depending on your particular tax circumstance.

Our projection is that our peak repurchase obligation will be about 30% of our free cash flow, which is typically less than the tax rate we would normally expect for our size company. Of course, this will vary depending on economic conditions, but it illustrates the point well. That being said, earlier in our history, our tax obligations would have been less because we were deploying a leveraged buyout strategy, which would've reduced our taxable income.

It's important to assess your own financial circumstances and risk tolerance when analyzing how much tax savings may be utilized to help fund your repurchase obligation.

At HB Global, we've deployed cash from our tax savings into growth and investments that generate returns for us. We're more focused on growing our free cash flow, but depending on your risk appetite, you may set this cash aside into an account dedicated to repurchase obligations.

Ability to Leverage Debt

While I understand that the worry over repurchase obligation is legitimate and that a lot of planning needs to go into ensuring a company has sufficient resources to buy back shares that become due, it's important to remember that there is debt capacity to pay this as well.

Very rarely does somebody buy another company worth tens of millions of dollars with all cash. Most people just don't have those resources sitting around, and they need to make the ownership transition by taking out debt and paying it off over a period of years. Why would an ESOP be any different? Why wouldn't it be appropriate at certain times to take out a reasonable level of debt to meet a repurchase obligation going through a peak?

That being said, as we talked about in my last soapbox, our appetite to take on debt is typically tied to our risk tolerance.

How This Plays Out at HB Global

I don't mean to sound cavalier about how I view repurchase obligation. It is a legitimate consideration that is crucially important to account for to ensure that distributions can be made to former employees and that the company can continue as a going concern. A person's view on repurchase obligations typically aligns with their risk tolerance.

Even internally, individuals within our company have different risk tolerances and view this differently. As our company has grown, some of our team members have put more focus on our repurchase obligations. My view is that our repurchase obligation is still relative to the size of our business. As our operating profit increases, our repurchase obligation increases, but the cash that we have to cover that repurchase obligation also grows as our profitability increases. The multiple for the value of a business relative to the free cash flow is an important number.

I certainly wouldn't want to try to operate an ESOP that has multiples of free cash flow similar to a high-growth tech company. It would be nerve-wracking to have to grow free cash flow at the rate needed to keep up with the prices of those tech companies. But when you have a relatively mature business with relatively stable cash flows that is valued in an economical and rational way, it's easier to manage repurchase obligations by monitoring them relative to your free cash flow and growth levels.

At HB Global, as our share price has grown, so has our free cash flow to support the increases in the repurchase obligation. While I have a relatively high risk tolerance, our Chief Financial Officer approaches things more conservatively and has a bit more angst over repurchase obligation. This leads to a healthy balance of risk tolerance within our organization. To reflect this balance, we perform stress tests, and we have a money market account set up that houses enough cash for our highest projected level of repurchase obligation over the next five years. These projections give everyone peace of mind because this ensures that we would have the resources needed to fulfill the repurchase obligation if debt markets totally froze. There is always a risk for a lack of liquidity in the system, and we need to be prepared for that situation and a reduction in free cash flow happening simultaneously. This has been a prudent strategy for us. Our first year of needing to fulfill our repurchase obligations came in 2020, and we all know what happened that year. In spite of that, we've never had any concerns over fulfilling this commitment.

While risk tolerance varies from person to person, the risk profile of the business will also change over time. As we talked about in the previous soapbox, our business is less risk-tolerant than it used to be. We now have people's entire retirement savings on the line that we don't want to put in jeopardy.

All of these are considerations we make when thinking about repurchase obligations. While it's an important component of being an ESOP that needs to be understood and accounted for, it needs to be understood from all perspectives, not just the perspective of what could go wrong. Knowledge is power. Cash production can be complicated, and repurchase numbers can be daunting. People tend to fill in what they don't know with negative assumptions. It's important to understand the impact of your decision on how it impacts not just the theoretically large, anticipated future value of company cash flows, but the impact it has on your employees and the benefits they receive as both retirement plan participants but also the beneficial owners of the company's equity. ESOPs generate alpha for their employees, which creates immense good in their lives and has the potential to ripple into the communities as well.

Another Perspective – Steven Ruether

Let's hear from Steven Ruether, former owner of the Bell Company, who decided to sell his company to HB Global in 2021.

1. What were your priorities when selling your company?

The history of the Bell Company, based in Rochester, NY, began with a plumber, John P. Bell Sr., who taught his family the plumbing and mechanical trade. His family included seven sons and one daughter who all worked together in the Rochester/upstate NY area. The family worked together (and fought together) and from those early years grew into one of the large nationally recognized Mechanical/Plumbing companies in the Eastern United States. The company took on many risk-related challenges that included high-risk type projects, such as hospitals, federal projects, nuclear-related projects, and, for a time, responsibilities as a major General Contractor. The strength was in the Mechanical/Plumbing, and we returned to our roots in 2008. The importance of this in regard to the sale of the Bell Company was that HB came in as a predominant mechanical firm, based on the number of other companies under the HB umbrella. The priorities for the sale were that Bell leadership and employees would be able to remain in control of our projects, relationships, and how we went about producing our projects. Our priorities included how we managed our projects and our conservative nature for handling risks in producing results. Bell had a structure for helping our project teams to produce the job, following long-standing policies for controls within each job we were awarded. Our process was to create simplicity for the project teams by utilizing controls on materials, subcontractor management, and labor man-hours, not so much in dollars and cents, but in regard to productive manhour reports for quantities installed over teaching craft/supervision quantity performance based on dollars and cents. Additionally, we rely on our project staff to be astute in scope of work and subcontract relationships (over strong management ideals). HB agreed with our processes and how we performed our work. Our history of projects during the negotiations showed our results. Without HB's agreeing to our method or madness of how we manage our projects and organization, our success under the HB logo may not have given the results Bell continues to produce. Our relationship with HB's staff is outstanding, and we believe the combination of HB and Bell will be successful for many years to come.

2. How did it feel selling your company to an ESOP?

Within the design and construction industry, Bell has been exposed to ESOP organizations. We felt the opportunity would greatly help in recruiting and maintaining personnel to help the Bell Company. As everyone knows, you have to have the employees, key management, support office personnel, and internal processes to be successful. Now, with being a part of HB and under the ESOP program, all of our employees are part of the win process. Construction work has many risks, and those risks are averted when employees know that labor, material control, subcontract management, safety, and quality within projects are critical. The ESOP gives all employees the opportunity to receive additional earnings by producing projects and following the policies and procedures that Bell has had for over 50-60 years. It is important to not so much brag about the value of ESOP but to relate to each employee that they make a difference each day they are working towards successful projects. Bell employees understand success comes from their performance.

3. How would you describe the success and legacy of your business today?

Going back in time, I'm reminded of the days past with the Bell family, made up of seven boys and one girl, in which each was ready to back each other up should a problem arise. (Stories were told of certain situations where the boys would sort of put the gloves on!) Our success has increased with joining HB and our other team of Brothers under the HB logo. Our growth has increased, with the opportunity to see how other HB firms operate and also to assist them as well. The HB groups may perform differently, but I would hope that as things move ahead, we each will learn how to improve in performance. Following up to question #1, performance of the work is key to success, and the controls on a project, however they are performed, should be simple and easy for any craft employee to see and feel that he has helped in the success of all the companies. I believe the Bell Company will continue to have success by following our long-ago developed processes and following the Bell Company unofficial rules of "Work Hard, Play Hard, and Treat all People Fair!"

Chapter 9
The Culture of Employee Ownership

The value we've created and shared with our employees has been the greatest source of pride in my career. However, my passion for employee ownership was fueled by a pivotal experience early in my career. This story is not a source of pride for me but one that has deeply shaped my perspective.

In my early 30s, I was in business for myself as a consultant. I had actually originally started my business to serve one particular client. While I was servicing this client, they acquired another company who had another service provider. When the acquisition was completed, my partner and I took on the work of the previous provider for the newly acquired business.

When the time came to decide how much to charge our client, my partner and I had different perspectives. My partner felt that we should charge the same amount the previous service partner was charging the acquired business in addition to the amount we were previously charging our client. We would just add the two fees together and charge that amount. I knew there had been some synergies created in the acquisition, and my gut told me that we should be cutting the fees to account for these synergies. I allowed my partner's perspective to win the day, and we charged what had previously been charged with no fee reductions.

Eventually, our client – who had treated us very well, by the way – saw right through this. They perceived us as not being fair, and we eventually lost the client over this. We lost the client that had been the reason I originally went into business for myself. The worst part wasn't the monetary loss of the client, but it was the other factors that played into the outcome.

I knew deep down that we should've reduced those fees, but instead of following my gut, I allowed myself to be persuaded. I didn't blame my partner, but rather took accountability for the fact that I knew what was right and didn't act on it.

More importantly, this story is pivotal in how I lead our business today. It's a big reason why I was so passionate about employee ownership in the first place. I'm a big believer in being fair, being transparent, and the principle of "the more you give, the more you get." How I approached that client situation was not aligned with my own personal mission and values. I didn't ever want to repeat that same mistake going into the future. This has shaped our business today.

We've created over $250 million worth of wealth at HB Global. I could think about how much of that I could've personally captured as a CEO if we hadn't formed an ESOP. But the amount of value we've created and shared is my greatest professional pride. Getting the report of how much value has been created and shared with our employees each year is like my Christmas. I've frankly done better financially than I could've imagined in my wildest dreams, and now I get to share $250 million of value with others who dedicate so much of their time and energy to their craft.

Forming an ESOP wasn't a goal I originally had when I bought HB McClure, but when I learned about it as a way to fulfill some tactical needs, it aligned exactly with what I wanted our company culture to be – one based on team and trust, where we could share in what we created and have a great place to work. An ESOP is a great way to create a culture that is people-focused, rooted in a foundation of trust, and is a place to work that people are proud of.

How an ESOP Benefits Culture

One of the main ways to enhance a culture and make it a great place to work is to give the employees a reason to want the organization to succeed. This doesn't necessarily mean that the employees need to share in the outcome, but they need to be emotionally tied to the outcome in some way. While the tie doesn't need to be monetary, however, a financial component is a material, concrete way to tie employees into the success of the organization.

While there are a variety of ways financial incentives can be used to tie employees to the success of the company, an ESOP is a structure tailor-made for doing this that benefits all levels of employees. It's not just executives getting long-term incentive plans. ESOPs allow employees throughout the organization to share in the success of the company. This is important because each employee is necessary for the business to thrive, not just the leadership team.

Many businesses will take the tack where leadership feels they're paying employees a good wage and that employees should want to work hard because of that. That usually gets old after a while. The cynicism of motives is still there when employees feel like they're just working for someone else.

An ESOP, on the other hand, aligns employees with the concept of the greater good. It gives employees multiple different ways to be emotionally tied to the success of the company. The concept of an ESOP is that when the company succeeds, individual employees succeed, and vice versa. Employees may be invested in the success of the company for their own financial gain. They may be passionate about helping to create value for their teammates. Providing the best possible service to the customer may be what gets them out of bed in the morning, which eventually creates superior financial results to be shared throughout the organization. ESOPs mitigate the mindset of "what's in it for me" and amplify a feeling of being united in a common cause.

Because of this emotional tie to the success of the company, we frequently see examples of employees going the extra mile. One of my favorite stories is about a service technician in Harrisburg. Our customer had a piece of HVAC equipment that needed to be replaced, and their business was shut down until this fix happened. Our service tech drove two hours after the end of their normal workday to get this piece of equipment. He then drove back two hours, and instead of waiting until the next day, he went to the customer's location and replaced the part so that when our customer came to work the next day, they were up and running.

We probably gained a customer for life because of that. While this behavior of going the extra mile definitely exists outside of ESOPs, I think employees should be rewarded for doing that. And from an employee perspective, the ESOP structure sparks a lot of emotional ties when deciding whether or not to go the extra mile. Because this employee went the extra mile, 1) we probably gained a customer for life that will continue to generate value for us, 2) that customer will likely tell others in their business community that could generate future value, 3) the value we create is ultimately shared back with that service tech, and 4) the service tech created value that is also shared with the team that they work alongside each day.

There are examples of this throughout our business. We see our team in the South work through hot and humid conditions in the summer, armed with loads of Gatorade. We see our team in the North fight their way through sleet, snow, and wind in the winter cold. Every employee gets to be tied to the fruits of their labor in an ESOP, and to me, that's the ultimate show of respect from an employer to an employee.

Longevity of ESOPs

Responsibility is my number one strength according to my Strengths Finder assessment from *Strengths Finder 2.0: A New and Upgraded Edition of the Online Test from Gallup's Discover Your Strengths* by Tom Rath.[50] I feel a responsibility to our employees that we do what we say we're going to do. As an ESOP, we say we're going to allocate shares over time to help each employee save for retirement. We can only do that as long as our business is sustainable.

If the longevity of the business is a priority for you, transitioning to an ESOP is a great option to consider because it structurally lends itself to sustainability. Longevity comes into play no matter how you want to exit an ESOP.

From a logistics perspective, the loans utilized in the process of selling to an ESOP trust are often structured for the long term, even 40 to 50 years. That itself implies that the company has the stability to be around for the long haul. If, instead of selling to an ESOP trust, you decided to sell to an ESOP company, it's probable the company will inherently have a growth mindset and the stability that is typically foundational in a successful ESOP.

More than that, people value the culture of the ESOP. The average tenure at HB McClure is nine years, and we see similar average tenures across our subsidiaries. These are reduced usually due to the growth of the company and the need to hire new employees, not by employee turnover. This isn't just unique to HB Global. In the 2022 survey of S-Corporations by the National Center for Employee Ownership (NCEO), 79% of respondents felt they were "much better than most" or "somewhat better than most" at the rate at which they recruited and retained employees relative to their competitors.[51] Employees value the way in which the company saves for their retirement with no contribution required from their side.

Furthermore, employees benefit from their own personal longevity at the company. The longer they are with the company, the longer their

[50] Tom Rath, *Strengths Finder 2.0* (Gallup Press, 2007).

[51] "S Corporation ESOPs" (PDF), National Center for Employee Ownership.

ESOP balances are able to compound. On top of that, ESOP allocations are made based on a percentage of the employees' compensation, so in theory, the longer the employee is with the company, the more they'll make, and the bigger the piece of the allocation pie they'll receive.

Moreover, evidence that points to the longevity potential of ESOPs is shown in the rate at which layoffs occur at these companies. In that same 2022 NCEO survey of S-Corporation ESOPs, respondents had an average annual involuntary separation (layoff) rate of 3% in 2021 as compared to 11.6% of non-ESOP companies, which shows the sustainability of these companies through the pandemic.[52]

Longevity is a mindset, though. Our leaders understand that having one good year won't produce a retirement for our employees. We have to do what we do and do it well day after day, year after year. We aren't working in spurts (which I believe is sometimes easier), but instead we're in it for the long haul. We need to balance a sense of urgency on what's important with a perspective that this is a marathon and not a sprint.

The last point I'll make on longevity is the ease with which the business can be transitioned. In a family business, the ESOP can more easily be transferred from one generation to the next without the next generation having to complete a huge buyout. For other non-family businesses, the next generation of leadership is able to assume leadership roles without buying out the current leadership. This makes the longevity of a business over generations of time more feasible.

Forming an ESOP isn't an instant guarantee of longevity, but it definitely provides the ingredients to help create a more sustainable company for generations if that is your goal as an exiting owner.

Mission and Core Values

Culture is not formed by being an ESOP alone. There are other factors that contribute to the company culture, which help create trust between

[52] "S Corporation ESOPs" (PDF), National Center for Employee Ownership.

employees and leadership that the success of the company is being fairly shared. Mission and core values are great ways to set and communicate culture in a company. But we don't want to just establish and communicate cultural guideposts; we want to truly scale our culture through all facets of the business and new facets of the business as our business grows. That is one of our top priorities in putting people first.

Earlier I mentioned that I worked for Continental Medical, where the mission, vision, and core values were present in all that we did. Selecting employees was based on our mission and core values. Performance reviews were done in the context of our mission and core values. Day-to-day and major decisions were made in the context of our mission, vision, and core values. Because this was a formidable time in my career, the impacts of this stuck with me.

As you know, I also worked for a company where core values, mission, and vision were not the focus. Having worked at companies that were on both extremes of the culture spectrum, I understood the importance of communicating and living up to the culture that we put in place as I came into HB McClure.

When I bought HB McClure, the core values were Trust, Quality, and Value. As we transitioned to an ESOP, our core values changed to align with that evolution, while recognizing foundational aspects of the business, such as trust. We have evolved to our mission now, which is to empower employee owners to make HB Global a great place to work and create value. This is supported by our core values of Trust, Team, Grit, and Growth. Our goal is to make our mission, vision (which we'll talk about later), and core values prevalent throughout our company. When employees see actions, communication, and language aligning with these values, we establish more trust that we are sharing fairly in the success of our company.

While core values and mission are important cultural components to establish, there are aspects of culture that exist outside of these guidelines and are instead captured as part of everyday actions and language. For example, decentralization isn't a core value of ours or stated in our mission, but it's an important component of our operations. I believe decentralization is embedded in a great place to work and helps to create autonomy. It's who we are and how we operate. We have our HB

Global level core values, but we encourage each subsidiary to establish additional core values specific to their business that still align with our overall mission and values. We allow our subsidiaries to operate in a way that makes the most sense for them because this will differ based on region, services offered, and leadership teams. Some subsidiaries are family-run, some subsidiaries are cost-focused, and some subsidiaries will naturally differ in their cultures because of their geographic locations. These differences in culture help make each of those subsidiaries a great place to work while still aligning with our overall mission and core values.

Despite the importance of decentralization to us, you won't find it plastered around our company. It's simply embedded in the actions that we take each day to *support* our mission and core values. When evaluating culture, be sure to evaluate the whole package.

To address this nuance, our company has developed a principles document as well. This captures some of the aspects of our business and culture that are crucially important but can't be captured in small sound bites like our mission and core values. In fact, decentralization is one of those principles. This document equips our leadership to scale the culture to their teams and gives all employees an easy reference document to create clarity in ambiguous situations. Furthermore, by capturing nuance outside of more established cultural guideposts like mission and core values, we have flexibility to adapt these as our business grows and changes.

As you consider exiting your company, it's important to consider your company culture. Are your values currently aligned with those of an ESOP structure? Do you have aspirational values that an ESOP structure would help facilitate? If you're looking to sell to an ESOP company, do your values align with those of a potential buyer? While culture is intangible, it's my belief that it's the most important thing.

On My Soapbox – Culture Is the Most Important Thing

If we figure that a career starts somewhere between ages 18 and 22 and lasts until somewhere between ages 59 ½ and 70, that means we could work from about 40 years on the short end to about 50 years on the long end. I don't want to feel unfulfilled and disengaged for that period of time, and I don't want the people I work with to feel that way either. I want to enjoy going to work each day and enjoy the people I work with.

Company culture is really about assembling a group of people who share what's most important to them and are aligned in a way that they enjoy working together. Team is important to HB Global and to me personally. I'll admit that I'm judgmental about selfish behavior. It drives me nuts. I don't want to work with somebody where it's all about them. Being a great teammate doesn't mean that it can never be about you, but it's recognizing that there's a time and a place and that we operate in a team structure. I want to work with people who care about how the decisions they make impact others.

Grit is another core value at HB Global. It's about doing what it takes when things get hard. Everyone has their own pet peeves. If grit is important to someone, it drives them crazy when they're around people who think it's too much work when things get a little bit challenging.

Culture is about assembling a team that shares the same values and enjoys working together because of this alignment. Because we're all unique as human beings, each culture will be different. It's necessary to recognize that "being a great place to work" is different for everyone. It's important to communicate what it means for *your place of business* to be a great place to work, create teams aligned with that, and allow team members who aren't aligned to select out of that culture.

According to Harvard Business Review, we spend about ⅓ of our lives – or more than 90,000 hours – working.[53] I surely don't want to be miserable for that time, and I don't want to be party to having others be miserable for that period of time. That's why it's important to communicate values and priorities and act on them. That's why culture is the most important thing.

[53] Dan Cable, "What You Should Follow Instead of Your Passion, Harvard Business Review, hbr.org, November 24, 2020, https://hbr.org/2020/11/what-you-should-follow-instead-of-your-passion?tpcc=orgsocial_edit&utm_campaign=hbr&utm_medium=social&utm_source=twitter.

Another Perspective – Matt Benner

Let's hear from Matt Benner, Commercial Plumbing Operation Manager, who has been with HB Global for 26 years, for a different perspective on ESOP participation.

1. *What does employee ownership mean to you?*

   It means the company is helping invest in my long-term future. I can have a larger impact on the company's success and benefit from it. The more I put in, the more we can all succeed together and not just benefit one owner, which leads to long-term financial stability.

2. *What impact has being part of an ESOP had on your life?*

   It has helped create a safety blanket for me and my family. It allows us to invest in our retirement without directly contributing our own money. As a manager, it has helped me engage employees by sharing the company's financial results, along with giving them a goal on the projects they can directly affect.

3. *How would you describe the culture of working at an ESOP?*

   It has created an improved team atmosphere and engagement for all our employees. We are all working towards one goal to create value for ourselves and everyone around us. Together, we can all have an impact on the future of the company and our retirement.

Chapter 10
Employee Engagement

One of the decisions that I'm most proud of in our entire 15-year ESOP history was our commitment in early March 2020 to our employees that we were going to pay their bonuses at the end of the fiscal year based on what we had achieved at that point rather than factoring in what impact the pandemic would have on future performance. Whatever happened for the rest of the pandemic year wouldn't come into play. That was a time of immense uncertainty and financial insecurity. Nobody had any idea what was going to happen or if we'd even be working. But it was important to us to provide any sort of certainty that we could to our employees, so we committed to paying out the level of the bonuses for the year that they'd achieved before the pandemic hit.

Our first instinct as a company was to ask the question of what we had to do to take care of our employees. The decision wasn't made solely by me; it was made by our entire leadership team. It was very courageous to make that decision when that could be capital that we would need to sustain our business. But if things got really bad, it was important to us to sustain our employee base. And we had full support from our division presidents for this decision. Some of our leadership team and division presidents were previous owners of businesses that were acquired by us, and some even had their earnout from the purchase that we'd done affected.

It turns out that this didn't end up making a big difference. For the most part, our financial results were not negatively affected, and we had the support of government programs such as the Paycheck Protection Program (PPP). We did end up paying out slightly higher bonuses than we would've without this commitment, but nothing major. The important thing, though, was that we made the commitment to our employees during a time of extreme uncertainty.

It's these types of situations that test us as an organization. It tested our decision-making ability. Could we make decisions with a long-term lens instead of just focusing on the short-term? It tested our priorities. Our people are our top priority. We kept our focus on our people before worrying about profits to generate the capital we may need for our company.

While there may be a slow adoption curve when selling to an ESOP, doing the right thing day in and day out to show that you are truly focused on employee engagement will make a difference in the rate and strength of adoption. These actions are both big and small. While our COVID bonus commitment was a big action, most times it's the little things that add up over time. Becoming an ESOP will not automatically make you employee-centric. You need to make a commitment to employee engagement to truly gain employee trust in the program and create a self-reinforcing cycle that bridges employees, customers, and profits.

The HB Global Vision

I believe there are three focuses that a company can have in the context of business: a financial focus, a customer focus, or an employee focus. In my opinion, two of the three work really well. The one that I don't think works really well is to make all your decisions through the lens of only caring about maximizing profits. When I started my career, I believed the North Star was to focus on maximizing shareholder value. That's what we were taught. While I do believe in maximizing shareholder value in the long term, I don't think that is attained by being focused on short-term financials or day-to-day operations.

For financially focused companies, I believe that many times they sacrifice the long term for short-term financial gains. The model of public companies puts a focus on the finances of these companies, especially in the short term, as the investment world is evaluating performance and projections quarterly. Besides sacrificing the long run for the short run, customers and employees also recognize that they're secondary in a financially focused company. I believe all of these lead to negative consequences for a business.

One model that I do think works well is being customer focused. This is one of the predominant models that is used by well-run companies. The customer is the North Star, and everything the company does is built around them. It's the purpose of the organization. Amazon is a great example of this that's played out over the last 25 years. Everything Amazon has done under the leadership of Jeff Bezos has been about the customer and the customer experience. Amazon Prime showcases a customer-centric offering that's played out really well for them.

There are, however, pitfalls to the customer-centric model. Because businesses become so intensely focused on the customer, there is the potential for the employees and suppliers to feel overlooked by the business. These are crucial players in the business ecosystem, but there are ways for companies to overcome these challenges while still keeping a customer focus.

The other model that I believe works incredibly well is an employee-focused model, and I think this is the least utilized of the three models. This is the one we deploy at HB Global. For us, being an ESOP and having an employee-centric model go hand-in-hand. We focus on what we can do to maximize employee engagement. Our vision then becomes focused on bridging what are traditionally competing ideas.

Our vision is that if we create engaged employees, the engaged employees will provide excellent customer service that creates raving fans, and our customers will be so satisfied that these raving fans will help us create superior financial results. These financial results are then shared back with our employees through bonuses and share allocations or are invested back into the company for growth that will eventually benefit employees. You can see how the cycle becomes self-reinforcing.

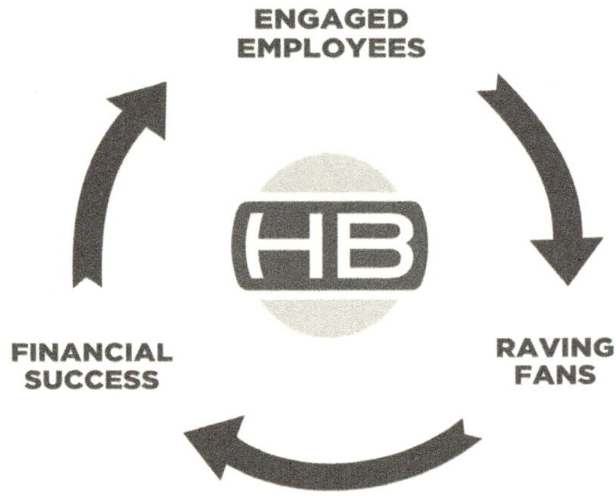

However, just like a customer-focused model, there are pitfalls to an employee-focused model. But, similarly, I believe these challenges can also be overcome. The struggle with this model comes from the individual employee level of what they feel the company should be doing to maximize employee engagement.

A more complex example I often reference is the commute time faced by our construction workforce. These employees like to do jobs that are close to their homes. Life is just better that way, plain and simple. But we don't always get to choose where the jobs we do are, and sometimes these jobs could be an hour and a half or two hours away. When we take these jobs, our employees often feel that we haven't made a decision in their best interest. The counter to that, however, is that if we don't take that work, our customer will end up working with our competition and may give more of their work, even local work, to that competition. This eats into the financial results that could be shared back with employees.

The connection isn't that simple, though. First of all, the financial results that employees see compound over time, so seeing the benefits of the work done on this long commute doesn't always come to fruition right away. Second, money isn't everything. Not everyone's experience is about money, and a certain portion of our employees would forego the money for more time at home.

All three models have challenges to overcome. We work to overcome the challenges of the employee-focused model by taking the time to explain decisions to our employees and really get their input on them. That, however, doesn't mean that every individual employee will buy into every decision. You just need to weigh the options.

Your Customer is Your Employee

For companies that utilize an employee-focused model, the leadership team's customer is the employee. If my vision is to put employees first, then I need to treat them as if they're my customers. While they're not the only constituency, they are the most important constituency if we say they're the highest priority.

As a CEO, the things I do in our business lend themselves really well to the employee being my customer. I'm not a construction expert. I can't value engineer a project to reduce the cost to our customer by putting in a different system. What I can do is push our teams to do that for our customers in a way that we're still a great place to work. My expertise lends itself to using my role as a CEO to make sure our decisions are aligned with our commitment to our employees.

We can point to very concrete examples of how we've done that. The first and most impactful way we put our employees first was the decision to become an ESOP and what that's produced over the last 15 years. Another example is that there hasn't been one subsidiary in our organization where our employee base shared in the short-term as much as what we've created going forward. In other words, in every subsidiary, we've paid out more in bonuses after the acquisition than were paid prior to that. The last example that I'll point to is the COVID bonus story that we opened the chapter with.

As an ESOP, it's important to make decisions that put your employees first in order to build the trust that you are in fact fairly sharing the success of the company. Building up this goodwill with employees makes a big difference in how effectively the ESOP model works. This takes time, though, by doing the little things and the big things in the best interests of the employees over time.

Going ESOP Isn't a Quick Fix

Becoming an ESOP isn't a quick fix for establishing a trusting culture that is dedicated to the mission and vision of the company. There are a couple of reasons for this. First, it takes time for ESOP balances to accumulate and employees to retire in order for the employee base to really buy into the financial benefits. The second is that we know that if we weren't making employee-focused decisions each day, we wouldn't have the culture that we have today in our organization, which is aligned with our mission, vision, and values.

From our experience, there is a slow adoption curve when transitioning to an ESOP. When we did this back in 2010, I was totally excited. I thought it was the greatest thing we could possibly do for our employees. We announced the transition to our employees before any shares were allocated, and not surprisingly, they did not feel the immediate passion that this was the greatest thing since sliced bread, like I did. Not surprisingly, our employees weren't super fired up about this like I was. However, we've seen that as those initial $600 balances grow and people watch their colleagues retire comfortably, we get more and more buy-in to what we're doing. But it didn't happen overnight.

There's also certainly a portion of our employees who would prefer more cash in their hands right now as opposed to it being placed in a retirement account. My take on it is that these employees are going to be extremely thrilled with that account balance when it comes time for them to retire. What we're doing as an ESOP is essentially forcing delayed gratification and discipline in saving. This also allows those balances to compound over time and grow more than if we handed over the capital right away.

For this system to work, there has to be a certain level of trust and goodwill that is built up with employees. We can't just implement an ESOP and hope they assume we have their best interest at heart and that it will work out one day. We make big and small decisions each day in their best interest to generate this trust and build a culture that is aligned with the shared purpose of an ESOP. We explain the decisions that we make so employees understand how it impacts them. It doesn't just matter what we do in an ESOP, but it matters how we do it.

It Doesn't Only Matter What You Do, But How You Do It

When my kids were teenagers and navigating the transition between us as parents needing to take care of them and them learning to take care of themselves, we used to have conversations that would revolve around helping them prepare to take care of themselves by making sound decisions. When we'd have these tough conversations, I'd always start with the question, "Do you trust that my only motivation is what's best for you?"

Because if they thought my motivations in the conversation were about me or how I want others to view the situation from the outside, we had a problem. They would not be responsive to my advice or dictate – whatever the situation called for – because we wouldn't be operating from a place of trust.

If I started with this one simple question, I could get their buy-in before the conversation even started to ensure they trusted that my motivation was in their best interests. The more they bought that, the more productively we could talk about whatever the topic at hand was, like why you shouldn't be able to go out until 2 a.m.

While this served me well in parenting, I think it's important in the business world as well to establish that level of trust. People are constantly making assessments of what your motivations are, and they'll give you a lot more slack if they trust that you care about them and the organization as a whole.

I actually have similar conversations today within our business where I'll ask our leaders or employees if they trust that my motivation is what's best for them and the organization. If they think that I'm prioritizing my own intentions, they're not going to trust some of the decisions I make. But if we can both approach a decision with trust that each party has what's best for the organization as their motivation, a productive dialogue can take place. We may not always agree on the tactics of what's best for the business, but we can trust each other's motivations.

There were times earlier on in our company where I would just flat out say, "Hey, this isn't in my best interest personally, but this is the approach I think we should take." It helped me to get the buy-in organizationally to take the strategies that I thought would be of most benefit to our company as a whole.

Building this trust is incredibly important. If we don't do this and our employees don't trust the motivations of leadership, they will try to fill in the blanks of our decisions on their own. Building trust is the reason that I spend a lot of time explaining decisions.

I recognize that we won't ever have 100% trust from every person in the organization, but there are things we can do to increase that trust. As an ESOP organization, it's crucial that the employees trust the motivations of management so we can maintain our shared purpose and all move in the same direction. While we may not be aligned on every decision, if we approach these decisions from a place of trust, it goes a long way in maintaining employee relationships and buy-in.

On My Soapbox – Put Your Money Where Your Mouth Is

One of the big things that we battle in an ESOP is the relationship between the employee and the employer. I believe that, in general, people don't trust the motivations of the businesses they work for and the leadership team. We start from a position where companies are distrusted by their employee base because people generally believe that people in power will utilize that power for their own benefit. As an ESOP and employee-centric business, it's important to put your money where your mouth is and ensure that your actions and behaviors align with what you articulate your culture to be.

Employees are really astute at seeing inconsistencies between actions and words. They come into a company with their radars up to spot these inconsistencies because they're cynical of the motivations of leadership. It's important to be conscious of aligning actions and behaviors with the words you're using to articulate your culture.

The catch is that there are always gray areas. For example, employees will perceive a layoff as not being employee-centric. It certainly is not employee-centric to the employees who are being laid off. However, it may very well be the best thing to do for the employees as a whole. For example, it's not good for the entire employee population to pay a bunch of people to sit around because there isn't enough work to keep everyone busy. Another example would be shutting down a division or a department. That's certainly not good for those being laid off, but the decision is made for the good of the broader employee base. Being employee-focused means focusing on the good of the whole and not necessarily every single individual employee.

Making employee-focused decisions when there's low-hanging fruit helps to build and maintain trust when those tough decisions come along. Safety is a great example in our company. Safety is the most important thing. I want all our employees to go home to their families in the same way they came to work that day. That is the basis for all our decisions. But if we were focused on safety for the purposes of saving money, our employees would be able to sniff that out right away.

Building up this trust and goodwill by taking aligned actions each and every day is also needed when a poor decision is made. Look, we're all human. Even though we're employee-centric, sometimes we will make a bad call. And even if it was unintentional, a bad call erodes trust. Then we just need to keep trying to get a little bit better each day by taking actions aligned with that employee focus to build that trust back.

There are a lot of things in an organization that I don't think work best when mandated by leadership. But when it comes to what you are as an organization, it's really important to start here. The leaders need to be aligned with what you articulate as your culture and need to set the example of behaviors that align with the culture. Words are just aspirational; behavior is where the rubber meets the road. Employees will take their cue on how to act from how leadership behaves.

Being employee-centric works both ways. Sometimes there will be decisions that employees don't view as being employee-centric, such as driving two hours to a job site, that benefit the organization as a whole. Sometimes there will be decisions that are very clearly viewed as being employee-centric but may not appear to be in the best interest of the organization in the short term. In both cases, using a lens of what will be in the best interest of employees and the company in the long term comes into play. It's the same concept as having two tails of risk.

In any case, if you're going to be an ESOP, you better be sure that you're prepared to align your actions with your words. Employees will sniff out if you have other motivations and if there's a disconnect between what you say you represent and what you actually do. Without unity of purpose and trust, the ESOP won't function to its maximum potential because it will lack engaged employees who are working to maximize the value being generated.

Another Perspective – Karl Heitzman

Let's hear from Karl Heitzman, a Warehouse Manager who has been with HB Global for 31 years, for a different perspective on ESOP participation.

1. What does employee ownership mean to you?

> Creating wealth entrusted by the employees, while seeking value that has direct interest in every single person within the organization.

2. What impact has being part of an ESOP had on your life?

> I've helped coach other employees that they have a direct interest in the value of the shares within the trust. Additionally, supplementing my retirement with this ESOP has given me a better balance for growth and income.

3. How would you describe the culture of working at an ESOP?

> Bringing energy towards a supportive team environment which allows us to clarify and communicate so we can make informed decisions on our everyday tasks.

Chapter 11
Unity of Purpose

In the early years of having bought HB McClure, my own personal mission as an executive evolved from being the leader of a great business to being a leader of employee owners. As that happened, that mission started to take shape in our business. We started to put into words what our company was about and now live by our mission to empower employee owners to make HB Global a great place to work and create value.

This mission is now regularly articulated throughout our company in written materials, in how we conduct our meetings, and on the walls of our offices. Having this mantra surround us serves as a continual reminder for us to make decisions through the lens of this mission. We strive to always act in a way that aligns with these words, and we challenge behaviors that are not aligned.

Our goal is always to make the best decisions for our employees as it relates to both making our company a great place to work and creating value that can be shared back with our employees. However, just because that's our goal doesn't mean there's always agreement. When we ask our employees to drive two hours to a job site, which causes them to be away from their family for a longer period of time, we've considered if this is in the best interest of our employees. It doesn't mean those employees necessarily agree. While we try to always make decisions that align with our mission, we're not perfect, but as time goes on, we move more and more into alignment with those ideals as we continue to live our mission and values.

As part of our mission, we're always striking a balance of making our company a great place to work without sacrificing value that can be shared back to our employees. It would be great if our customers wanted to pay us more because we're employee owned. But that's generally not the case. Customers want to pay us for the value we provide. We still need to operate within the laws of economics.

But being an ESOP makes striking the balance of generating value and taking care of our employees much easier than many other business structures because an ESOP creates a unity of purpose. The unity of purpose comes into play because our shareholders are our employees. While many businesses need to balance creating returns for outside shareholders with nurturing their employees and culture, an ESOP is taking care of its employees when creating value for the shareholders because this is one-in-the-same group. This helps us to better balance a focus on creating value with also taking care of our employees.

What Is Unity of Purpose?

I grew up playing sports and had a multitude of coaches over the years. I'm sure many of you share this experience. When you feel like you have a coach who's really working for your benefit to make you and the team better, you play harder, and the team comes together. But when you feel like you've got a coach who's out there to fulfill their own competitive needs and only cares about winning, you have a tendency not to want to play as hard or devote yourself as much to the team.

The same thing is true in business. Operating with a unity of purpose means we're all moving in the same direction. As leaders, we're creating and guiding teams for both the betterment of the employees and the success of the company. To really demonstrate this point, let's take a look at a couple of counterexamples.

A classic counter case is an employer that has a union in which the union and its members are more focused on what they want to achieve rather than what the business wants to achieve. The business and its members are moving in opposite directions, focused on what they think is best for themselves. This creates feelings of opposition rather than alignment, creating ripe opportunity for conflict and stagnation. On the other hand, there are also unions that work to be in alignment with the employer of their members, where each party is striving for mutually beneficial outcomes. This is unity of purpose.

Another example is likely one that we can all relate to. One day, my cable provider came to my house to do some work. For the hour that the technician was there, he did not speak highly of the company he was working for and talked about how he could take advantage of the company. Nothing he said was aligned with what the company was trying to do. While I can't be a fly on the wall in this company's leadership meetings, I'm willing to bet this tone starts there. This is an extreme case of separation of purpose, where the employee base is working against what the entity is trying to achieve.

As an ESOP, there is a natural unity of purpose built into the structure. As a management team, we are incentivized to get everyone highly aligned with what we are trying to achieve because it's not just good for us; it's good for everyone. On the flip side, given all employees own our business, they are highly incentivized to be aligned with what we're trying to accomplish. Everyone who's participating has skin in the game.

The adoption of this concept and the incentive to be aligned don't always happen right away. While there are some early adopters, many people have to see it work over time. We discussed earlier that the median ESOP balance of employee owners who have been with HB McClure since 2010 and are still with us today is $392,000. What is often forgotten is that the first contribution to these employee owners on October 1, 2011, was only $600... that they couldn't even access until retirement. This set of employees had to take a leap of faith. But their continued outstanding service is a testament to their recognition of the unity of purpose in our company.

Creating more opportunities like that for our employees is why we strive to get as many of our team members aligned as possible.

Leading with a Unity of Purpose

Unity of purpose isn't just dependent on employees buying into the mission of the company. As you can imagine, unity of purpose starts with leadership.

I view our employees as my business partners. On the one hand, there are a lot of things I excel at that are unique to my experiences that help me to lead the company effectively. On the other hand, there are a lot of unique skills that our employees possess that I don't have expertise in. The environment that an ESOP creates of us all working towards the same outcomes helps us to recognize all the unique things that our team brings to the table, not just what society recognizes as being unique.

When you invest money, there's an expectation of a certain level of return on your investment; with business owners, there's the same expectation. But we can't meet those return expectations without our labor, and my basic belief system is that we should share what we create with the labor that is enabling those returns. We can't be successful without every single person in our business, from our warehouses to our pipe hangers to our accounting team. We need each person, otherwise, they wouldn't be part of our company. Employee ownership recognizes that everybody should participate in the success we create. It fosters a unity of purpose because our laborers are our shareholders. As a leadership team, we aren't juggling between shareholder returns and taking care of our employees.

Employee ownership is also a way in which we can show respect for our employees. Sure, there are many ways employers can show their employees respect, but sharing the value that is created through the success of the company is a concrete way to do this. That's not always what society does. Hot dog and beer vendors at sporting events are crucial to the success of the organization, but the organizations aren't sharing value with those vendors to mirror that success.

Embracing Competing Ideas

In Jim Collins' book *Built to Last*, he discusses the "Genius of the AND." He explains, "Visionary companies do not brutalize themselves with the 'Tyranny of the OR' – the purely rational view that says you can have either A *OR* B, but not both.... Instead, they embrace the 'Genius of the AND' – the paradoxical view that allows them to pursue both A *AND* B at the same time."[54] Jim isn't just referring to ESOPs in his books. He's guiding leaders who want to create visionary companies. But as the leader of an ESOP, I think this concept of the "Genius of the AND" is particularly relevant to employee ownership.

It's difficult for people to keep two competing ideas together. There are varying degrees of difficulty. Some ideas, while potentially challenging to reconcile, are not impossible to unify. Ideas that seem to be contradictory on the surface may actually gain momentum when they are embraced with an attitude of "and" rather than assumed to be incompatible.

For example, treating employees well or striving for superior financial results are often seen as competing ideas, where you can do one or the other exceptionally well but not both. It's our job as leaders to show that these things can peacefully coexist. Although there is a financial cost to treating employees well, what's unseen is that there may be a performance increase in employees when they're treated well. Therefore, those two ideas that could seem counter to each other actually start to self-reinforce and lead to better results. We can acknowledge that there are other ways to do it, but we also recognize that we're so committed to this that we're going to behave in a way that's aligned with that.

[54] Jim Collins, *Built to Last* (Harper Business, 1994): 10.

Often, decisions that are made when embracing competing ideas are decisions that don't *have to* be made. Companies can get away with not making these decisions and fall back on the norm of incompatible ideas. But being a leader who embraces unifying competing ideas for the good of your company often means making the decision anyway.

In 2024, the financial results for HB Global were so exceptional that they surpassed the bonus programs that we communicated to our employees. As part of our bonus program, we provide a range for bonus potential based on defined performance tiers, but our 2024 results were above and beyond what we'd committed to for a max bonus payout to our employees. While we outline a formal bonus program, at its core, we view bonuses as a means to share a portion of the profits our employee owners help create. When we exceeded that program, we could've gotten away with just paying out the maximum stated bonus. Our employees probably would've still been thrilled with that. But we didn't stop there, we paid out bonuses above and beyond that max payout. We hadn't committed to paying above the performance tier ahead of time, but we made the decision to move forward with it anyway. To us, it was important to continue to share profits in the short term through bonuses in addition to the long-term ESOP program.

There are business reasons we could've used this excess cash in other ways, like paying down debt. This also would've benefited employees indirectly, but we made the decision to move forward with the bonuses because that decision aligned with our ideals. The right decisions don't always mean giving more; sometimes, there is a need to be more disciplined. But I firmly believe this decision will create momentum in generating superior financial results as an outcome of treating our employees well. That's not why we paid the bonuses, but it shows how two competing ideas can peacefully coexist.

Assume Positive Intent

Around HB Global, we use the phrase "assume positive intent." It's one of the behaviors we associate with our core value of Trust. Assuming positive intent creates an environment where unity of purpose and embracing competing ideas can thrive.

I ask our employee base to start with an assumption of positive intent. I want our employees to assume that of each other, and I want them to assume that of me. In all decisions I make, I'm making them from the perspective of what's in the best interest of the organization and our people. I know that all employees won't agree with 100% of the decisions I make, and frankly, they shouldn't. I know if I sat out at a project site all day, I wouldn't agree with every tactical decision being made either. But if we can all start from a place of trust and assuming positive intent, we open up the opportunity for dialogue where we can really talk about what's best.

We have some employees who are so obsessed with maximizing the material they have that they'll actually end up spending way more money maximizing that material than what they actually save. For example, some employees view it as prudent to buy material in bulk to get a discount despite needing to store the extra materials. Others view this as wasteful to have to dedicate extra resources to these materials that aren't needed right away to eventually spend time to go find these materials in a warehouse. Neither perspective is technically wrong; it all depends on perspective and circumstances, like how long it will take to use the material or what's going on in the supply chain. If I start from a position that the employee is trying to do the very best thing they can for the company, then we can talk about whether that tactical decision makes sense. We have trust in each other that we're just trying to get the best answer for the company. And that's unity of purpose.

For us, that's what we're trying to achieve. We will never get to 100% alignment, but our batting average will be a lot higher with the assumption of positive intent.

Assuming positive intent can, and should, take place at companies structured in any way. But an ESOP helps to facilitate this attitude because it naturally creates an environment of "we're all working towards the same goal." It's one of the reasons I'm passionate about advocating for the employee ownership structure.

Non-Financial Compounding

We all have a few concepts in life that we 100% buy into. Compounding is one of those concepts for me. We talked earlier in the book about financial compounding. That is the most concrete and tangible example of this principle, but it's my belief that nothing escapes this law.

Conscientiously doing the right thing day in and day out is one of my favorite examples of compounding. No matter what arena of life this is taking place in, it's going to compound over time and pay dividends.

Commitment to relationships is a great example. This can be any relationship in your life. Doing the right thing by the other person and being selfless in that relationship builds value in that connection. This compounds over time by consistently doing the little things right.

Just like the financial world, there can be setbacks as it relates to compounding. Doing the wrong thing in a relationship – whether intentional or not – can be catastrophic. If a misstep doesn't take the trust level to zero, it at least puts you further back, and then you need to work to earn that trust back.

This concept plays out throughout different areas of life. Wisdom is another great example. It's something that compounds over time through our experiences that build on each other. If we really take the time to assess our decisions and how they play out, we're building wisdom. But wisdom, like financial compounding, is not something that can be rushed. It has to play out over time through experience and reflection.

Athletics is another relevant example. According to Malcolm Gladwell, it takes about 10,000 hours to master a new skill. Yes, athletes can have a natural talent, but when they devote the hours to practice, that effort and natural skill compound to create more incredible talent and expertise.

In all areas of life, compounding happens by doing the right things day in and day out. They don't need to be big things. The little things will add up over time. At HB Global, I say that we want to try to be just 1%

better every day. That small, consistent effort builds on itself over time to create incredible results.

When you're starting an ESOP, there's a learning curve to it for both you as a leader and your employees. It takes time to figure out how to work together in this structure, and more importantly, it takes time to build the trust that is necessary for employees to believe that the success of the company is being fairly shared back with them and that leadership truly has their best interests at heart. As leaders, when we consistently show up to support our employees, ensure their safety on the job, and recognize that our employees have lives outside of their jobs, we show them a different level of respect. This trust and respect compound to show our employees a level of appreciation they deserve for the labor they contribute to our company's success.

On My Soapbox – Unity of Purpose in the Workplace and Beyond

I have conversations with employees about what we do here and what the most important things in their lives are. I recognize that these are two different things. Even for me, as the CEO, I don't describe my mission at HB Global as my biggest personal mission. It's my professional mission. My primary mission in life is built around my family.

When I have these conversations with employees, I talk about the importance of striking a balance between these two things. But balance isn't even really the right word; it's more of an integration because work and life outside of work are happening simultaneously. It's not like we can consciously create a 50/50 split. And the proportion of time and energy that we devote to each arena of our life will change day to day depending on what is demanding our attention at that particular time.

As leaders, it's important that we recognize and support a healthy work and life integration. This is another "and." While creating more balance in our personal lives may seem like a competing idea from increasing productivity, it's not. Supporting a healthy balance between work and personal life for employees typically leads to producing more and better outcomes in the long run. An unfortunate example of this is cases of divorce. You don't have to be around very long to see what going through a divorce does to people's productivity. In my entire career, of all the people I've worked alongside going through a divorce, I've only ever seen one person go through it without a material decrease in productivity.

More importantly, over the long run, I certainly don't want to be party to somebody waking up at 65 years old and wondering for whom and for what they did all that work. Frankly, that's where a lot of business owners end up… really financially successful but with nothing else that matters. That's not what I'm interested in for myself or for anybody at our company.

At 55 years old, I think I've done pretty well with this overall. Does that mean I've done it great every single day and every single moment? No, it doesn't. You can ask my wife, Mandy. Sometimes I get stuck in Bob's World, where my mind wanders to work matters during family time. She's really great, though, in giving me the grace I need when work is demanding more of my attention, and when she feels I need to snap out of it to turn my attention to a family matter, she gives me that feedback. And it's important that we accept that feedback from our loved ones, get engaged where we should be engaged, and give ourselves grace as we try to balance this integration.

As leaders, we also need to recognize that we set this tone. I take one vacation a year where I'm (almost) totally disconnected. I'm not checking emails or text messages. I give my phone to Mandy and tell my most immediate team members that if there's an emergency, they can call her on my phone. But it better be a real emergency…

I encourage all of our senior leaders to take at least one vacation where they are totally disconnected. Heck, if they want to take all their vacations that way, that's totally good by me. But I want to make it a point that they take at least some time to totally disconnect at least once a year. I don't enforce this, and some are better than others at doing it, but the tone is set. And that tone trickles throughout the organization.

Soon, that attitude of being productive at work "and" integrating personal lives becomes the norm throughout the organization. These two traditionally competing ideas start to self-reinforce to create a culture that is more productive with a home life that is more fulfilled. Employees appreciate this and reflect that in their work.

Unity of purpose runs deeper than financial and employee morale. It permeates all areas of our lives.

Another Perspective – Trevan Espenshade

Let's hear from Trevan Espenshade, a Construction Superintendent who has been with HB Global for ten years, for a different perspective on ESOP participation.

1. What does employee ownership mean to you?

Being an employee owner gives me excitement and purpose for the company's success. When the company succeeds, so do I. The profits don't go to sit in a CEO personal account; they go to the employees.

2. What impact has being part of an ESOP had on your life?

Being part of an ESOP gives me a peace of mind to know that I will have a nice account balance at retirement time with no out-of-pocket cost. This makes my retirement planning so much easier. Not having to put as much money into other retirement funds helps with extra money for monthly expenses.

3. How would you describe the culture of working at an ESOP?

Our culture screams accountability and quality in everything we do. If quality is poor, extra costs are associated, and we lose profits. Accountability is knowing that all our actions every day control the company's success and our own personal profit. It is a win-win for both the company and the employees when being in an ESOP.

Conclusion

In our 2025 annual meetings, the single most important slide I presented showed how the 80% increase in our share price in 2024 positively impacted the contribution of ESOP shares to each employee as a percentage of their pay. But that wasn't the most important part. What was most important actually came from our employees.

At each meeting, I asked them who was responsible for these results and contributions, and the response was the same in every group: "We are."

That was powerful. There was a recognition throughout all facets of the company that the entire company, each subsidiary, each team, each individual.... had the ability to impact our contribution percentage based on how successful we are in what we produce.

Yes, we were operating in a strong external environment in 2024, which helped strengthen our results, but the point is that we have something to say about the outcomes of the company, ultimately impacting each individual employee.

My message on employee ownership is simple: We all have a role to play. We can all make this happen. And the more we all commit to doing everything we can to help the company, the better we're all going to be. Employee ownership is what makes this model a reality.

Contribution, Not Control

Employee ownership creates a culture based on everyone sharing in what's created. In this culture, employees have a tendency to engage in what the entity becomes and have agency around making that happen. This is a definite contrast to the traditional model in which employees are subservient to a leader who is driving the entire company.

Don't get me wrong, I think effective leadership plays an important role in creating something great. But as important as proficient leadership is, it's not as important as the agency of the individual employees who have the power to create an exciting and vibrant working environment. The role of leadership becomes focused on inspiring the entire group to do great things and make the company the best they feel it can be. At HB Global, we have 1,700 people who can do great things. They can accomplish a lot more as a group than one leader or a senior leadership team can, no matter how effective those leaders are at making things happen.

The agency that's encouraged in an employee ownership structure may sound scary at first. It may seem like an environment ripe for anarchy, but the reality is that it creates a collection of people working together in a way where everyone is incentivized to do their best work towards a common goal. The agency involved in employee ownership doesn't mean that ESOPs operate in an every-person-for-themselves environment.

At HB Global, our 1,700 employee owners are spread throughout the country. We do have a hierarchical structure. We do have standards that the employees need to adhere to. We do have guidelines and processes in place to ensure safety and quality. But our employees still have agency. In our company, it starts with providing autonomy as close to the customer as possible and giving employees the autonomy to take on things that are appropriate for their role and scope. Because we want to create a culture based on agency, each supervisor is responsible for making this happen, which means autonomy cascades throughout the organization. As leaders, each supervisor is responsible for what they delegate to their teams and then – this is important – holding them accountable for the results. Only when there is execution and successful results is value created for each employee.

And here's why agency works. I've found that the more you allow people to find solutions, the more they take responsibility for the work they do. The more you direct people on how things should be done, the more they shirk responsibility. If I'm always directing the minutia of what should be done, that takes responsibility off of everyone else. But if I say that I trust that our employees have the skills and knowledge to work together to overcome a challenge, a lot more gets accomplished, and everyone feels more fulfilled.

In sports, athletes are typically more successful when they "play free." There's less thinking and more doing. That's in essence what agency allows for and what we're trying to do as a business. We want 1,700 employees to "play free" and have the opportunity to do what they know is in the best interest of the company without worrying about someone being all over them for making a bad decision.

Structure is important. Leadership is important. But I believe, on the whole, we overemphasize the importance of the leader and underemphasize the importance of the whole system. Employee ownership as a system reinforces the agency of the individual to make an impact on what a company is trying to do.

Some leaders may be afraid of what could happen if they give autonomy and something goes wrong. What I would say to them is that somewhere along the line, some leader inspired you by allowing you to stretch your potential. If we don't take risks – if we don't trust that our employees have the skills to figure it out – we don't reach our potential.

The American Experiment

Agency allows us to learn from our failures. Cultivating agency won't always lead to the right answer right away. Just like parents want their kids to learn from their mistakes instead of making their own, business leaders often want to shelter their teams from making mistakes – whether that's to protect their team members or to protect themselves. But part of learning and growing is that we need to get direct feedback ourselves.

As leaders, we have to let people learn from their mistakes. Of course, we allow this within reason. Maybe we have a tolerance of a few hundred dollars, or a few thousand, or maybe the team member is simply embarrassed. We don't allow mistakes that could put the company as a whole at risk or put anyone's safety at risk. We allow mistakes that encourage our teams to learn. Winners win, and they will take that feedback to fine-tune their future performance.

We allow these failures because these failures often lead to future successes. Technology in our society is a great example. We've had the technology breakthroughs and developments that we've had because people have had the agency to try different things, many leading to failure and some leading to massive success. Agency leads to innovation.

On a grander scale, this is the American experiment. The reward system works. When we produce innovation based on our agency, we are rewarded for it. Entrepreneurs who innovate successfully see fruitful financial results for their companies and for themselves. We're set up for innovation. Yes, that can lead to some disparities based on how we're set up now, but what if we made agency more widespread?

That's employee ownership. Employee ownership is creating agency at every level of our workforce. It allows entire groups to create and perform to their highest potential while working towards a common good. It's a way that we can increase the median income for the masses. It's a way for everyone to participate in the American dream.

Rooted in Intention

If you've made it to this point in the book, you believe in capitalism. You believe in the American experiment, and you believe in the American dream being accessible for the labor that makes our companies and country what it is.

For most people who have made it this far, if you take all the factors into consideration regarding what you want to accomplish out of the sale of your business, it will lead you to want to sell to an ESOP, whether that's creating an ESOP or selling to an ESOP strategic buyer. Transitioning to an ESOP creates a system that allows you to accomplish all the things for your business that we've discussed throughout this book: ownership transition, leadership transition (if desired), maintaining the legacy of the business, taking care of the employees who've helped you get to where you are, respecting the customer experience, and being a positive asset to your community.

All that being said, an ESOP is only valuable in creating these byproducts if you truly buy in to everything that's involved in employee ownership. If creating an ESOP is just a financial tool for you and your behaviors aren't aligned with employee ownership, your employees won't buy in, and the benefits of being employee-owned won't manifest.

Becoming an ESOP isn't a magic bullet to create financial success and a lively culture. Being successful as an ESOP requires not just making sound business decisions but aligning all your behaviors with having your employees' best interests in mind. That is how you will truly create value in this structure. With the right mindset, the benefits have the potential to be immense.

By selling to an ESOP, no matter what structure or transition path you choose, you're servicing your employees by building value for them through a retirement asset. You are keeping jobs and resources within your community. You are maintaining the legacy of your business. And you're creating a sustainable future for your company. This may not come at the highest purchase price, but in the end, if these are your priorities, the transaction will be a major success.

Looking Ahead

I've made a public commitment that our goal is to help each of our employees become millionaires in retirement. With our efforts since becoming an ESOP in 2010, we're on track to do that, and we continue to make decisions that align with what we need to do to achieve that.

While this is a big commitment, I don't shy away from it. Each year, some of our newer employees even go so far as to say that I sound like a "used car salesman" when I talk about this. While I now lean into this as a joke, I'm very serious about this commitment. And I'm serious about delivering what we promise.

There are two reasons I don't shy away from this commitment. The first is that I believe it's necessary to bridge the gap between what Social Security provides and what will allow our employees to maintain their standard of living in retirement. The second is that I understand the power of compounding. If we do the right things – big and small – over time, making millionaires of our employees is really not that big of a lift.

We're proud of the progress we've made since becoming an ESOP in making each of our employees millionaires in retirement. I've seen how this can play out. I've seen the success that is possible with an ESOP, and that's why I'm so passionate about business owners being aware of this structure as an option.

The chart on the next page demonstrates just how feasible it is for an employee to reach the million-dollar mark in their ESOP account. Here we assume a median wage of $81,640 with 3% yearly wage increases. We also assume the employer contributes 10% of annual compensation each year and that there is a 10% growth rate in the share price. With these assumptions, the employee can reach the million-dollar mark in 25 years.

This is a legitimate scenario that could work out for a 40-year-old technician who joins us and progresses through the company.

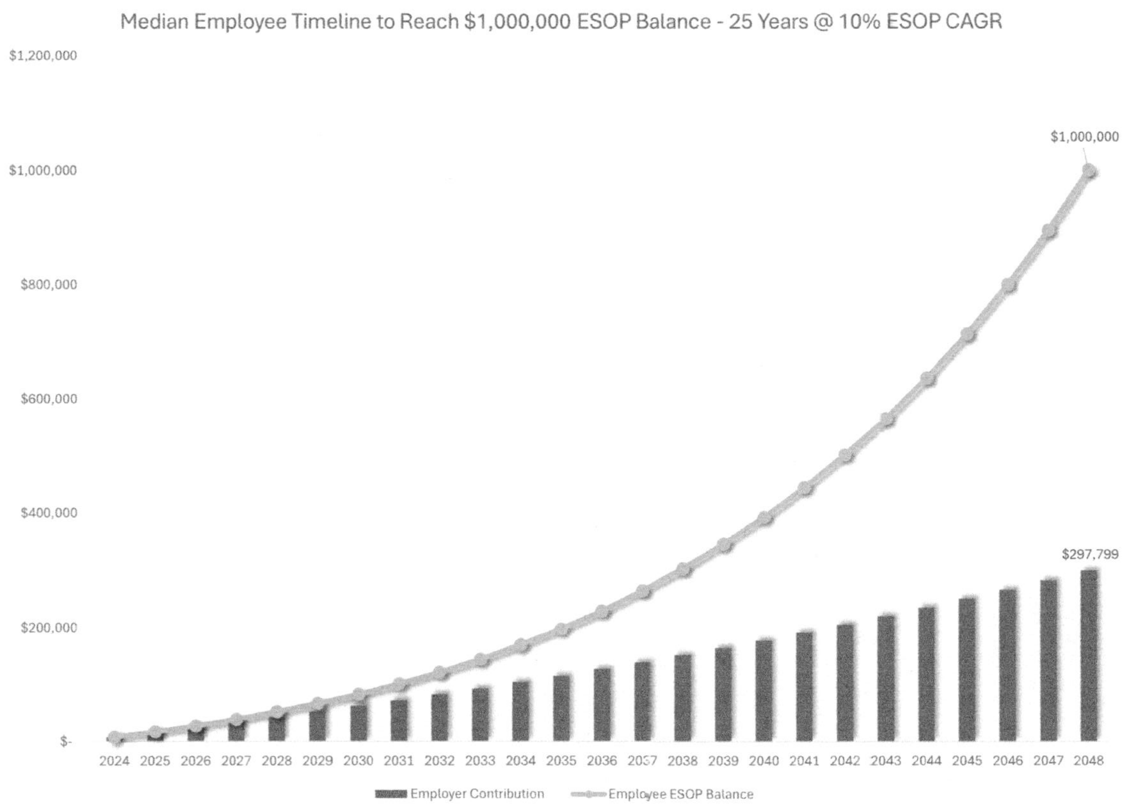
Median Employee Timeline to Reach $1,000,000 ESOP Balance - 25 Years @ 10% ESOP CAGR
$1,200,000
$1,000,000
$800,000
$600,000
$400,000
$200,000
$-
$1,000,000
$297,799
2024 2025 2026 2027 2028 2029 2030 2031 2032 2033 2034 2035 2036 2037 2038 2039 2040 2041 2042 2043 2044 2045 2046 2047 2048
Employer Contribution
Employee ESOP Balance

Go Forth

If this sounds too good to be true, it's not. It's why ESOPs are incentivized by the government and are one of the *very* few things that receive bipartisan support. ESOP companies create real value for their employees. On a broader scale, they also give employees a great sense of fulfillment... a sense that they have a say in the outcomes of their career and the impact they make.

You have the ability to make millionaires of your employees. You have the ability to create and keep resources in your community. You have the ability to leave a legacy and a business that is set up to sustain over the long term. An ESOP creates a system for this.

Any ownership transition is difficult to endure, but by choosing an ESOP, you create sustainable ownership in the future that benefits the labor that makes the company what it is. If you're looking to get rich quick, hop on your jet, and never look back at what happened to your company, an ESOP isn't for you. If you care about the people who helped you get there, the community that supported you along the way, and the legacy you leave behind, I invite you to seriously consider the ESOP structure.

Here's What to Do Next

This is just the beginning!

If you'd like to dive further into the world of ESOPs, here are a few ways you can take the next step:

1. Access Additional Resources

In the appendix, we've included a few additional resources that will help you learn more about ESOPs or connect to others in the field.

2. Explore Being Acquired by HB Global

If you feel that joining the HB Global family of brands might be a great fit for your company, visit our Acquisition page at https://hb-global.com/acquisitions/

3. Learn More About Our Approach to Being an ESOP

If you found the views and perspectives in this book helpful, there's more where that came from! Check out our Employee Ownership with Bob Whalen podcast series and blogs at: https://hb-global.com/articles/

4. Hire Bob to Speak

If you're looking for a speaker who embraces the power of story and experience to educate on ESOPs without making it feel like you're sitting in a lecture hall, I'd love to speak at your next event!

Email: beyondownership@hb-global.com with "SPEAKING" in the subject line.

Appendix: Additional Resources

In this appendix, you will find some additional resources that we find beneficial. This is not a comprehensive list, but a good place to get started!

Organizations

- National Center for Employee Ownership (https://www.nceo.org/)
- The Baker Project (https://bakerproject.org/)
- The ESOP Association (https://www.esopassociation.org/resources)

Additional Reading

- An Introduction to ESOPs (21st Edition): How an employee stock ownership plan (ESOP) can benefit your company, its owners, and its employees by Scott Rodrick
- Understanding ESOPs: A primer on employee stock ownership plans (2nd Edition) by Corey Rosen and Scott Rodrick
- Ownership: Reinventing Companies, Capitalism, and Who Owns What by Corey Rosen and John Case

Acknowledgments

I want to start by acknowledging all employee owners at HB Global. Without your dedication and determination, our ESOP would not be the success it is today. Because of you, we have been able to both create and share an immense amount of value with our teams. Beyond that, because you trust in the employee ownership mission and vision, we're able to not only grow employee ownership within HB Global, but we are also able to serve as a guide for how other companies can preserve their legacy and take care of their employees.

I would also like to thank the business owners who have trusted their businesses with us. Because you believed in our mission and our culture, we've been able to grow employee ownership faster than we otherwise would've been able to.

I'd especially like to thank Bob McClure for trusting me with the acquisition of his family's business, HB McClure Company. Although I came with different industry experience, you were able to see my passion for taking care of the employees of the business and continuing the legacy of the blue and gold. Although becoming an ESOP wasn't the original plan, that purchase was the beginning of this incredible mission of advancing employee ownership.

That being said, I'm also grateful to the 2010 HB McClure Board of Directors, who, while they thought I might be a little nuts for my decision to sell the company to an ESOP, trusted the vision that I had and supported the effort to become employee owned.

I'd also like to thank Mark Caldwell, who was the ringleader who got me into the business, and my uncle, Tom Whalen, who joined the board with me in 2008 and was an invaluable resource as I got my sea legs in the construction field.

I'd like to acknowledge all the teachers, coaches, and mentors who have helped shape my belief system. While there are too many to name, please know that I am grateful each day for the lessons and wisdom imparted to me over the years.

Last but certainly not least, I want to recognize my family, especially my parents, to whom I owe it all. Mom and Dad – your selflessness was an example to us all.

About the Author

Bob Whalen currently serves as the President and Chief Executive Officer at HB Global, LLC. Bob joined the HB Global family in 2009 as the first non-family member CEO of its legacy organization, HB McClure Company in Harrisburg, PA, which was established in 1914. Since then, HB Global has grown to be an ESOP holding company with subsidiaries across the United States focused on service, replacement, and construction in the commercial, residential, and infrastructure markets. Bob is passionate about making HB Global a great place to work and creating value for its employee owners.

Before joining HB Global, Bob worked in various positions and companies in the employee benefits space. In 1997, Bob started his own employee benefits consulting business, which he sold to Mercer in 2002. Additionally, Bob held various positions at Mercer over a five-year period before acquiring HB McClure Company.

Bob has a BS in Agricultural Economics and an MBA from Cornell University. He also earned an MS in Finance from the University of Notre Dame. Outside of work, Bob enjoys hunting, fishing, and golfing.

While Bob is passionate about ESOPs, his highest mission in life is his family. Bob is married to his wife, Mandy. They have four children and six grandchildren whom they adore spending time with and creating memories with whenever possible.

Made in the USA
Middletown, DE
09 August 2026

30658205R00117